NINJA FOODI GRILL

COOKBOOK 2021

250 Effortless Delicious Recipes
For Indoor Grilling & Air Frying

By

EMILY COOK

Disclaimer

Please note, the information written in this book, are for educational and entertainment purposes only. Strenuous efforts have been made to provide accurate, up to date and reliable complete information in this book. All recommendations are made without guarantee on the part of the author and publisher. By reading this document, the reader agrees that under no circumstances are we responsible for any losses, direct or indirect, which are incurred as a result of the use of the information contained in this document, including but not limited to errors, omissions or inaccuracies.

Table of Contents

Introduction to Ninja Foodi Grill

The Ninja Foodi Grill is a **kitchen appliance** used in cooking delicious and sumptuous meals. It is one of the latest additions to a growing community of Foodi products. In does not only grill it can also air fry, bake, roast, and dehydrate. The unit is big and boxy. The Ninja Foodi Grill is constructed of brushed stainless steel and has a black plastic domed lid. There's a grill grate, crisper basket, and a cooking pot which are coated with a ceramic nonstick finish.

The Ninja Foodi Grill as the name implies grill food with the lid closed. The lid doesn't press down on food but it only brands grill marks on one side at a time. The idea of the Ninja Foodi Grill air frying, bake, roast, and dehydrate makes it to overlap the normal Ninja Foodi Pressure Cooker and Ninja Foodi Oven.

However, the Ninja Foodi Grill is well constructed, the digital controls are easy to read and intuitive to navigate. It grills food excellently well without any smoke coming out from the unit.

Meaning of Ninja Foodi Grill

The Ninja Foodi Grill is a kitchen appliance used in cooking delicious and sumptuous meals. The unit circulates air around food for amazing Surround Searing and also the high-density grill grate creates food that's perfectly cooked on the inside and char-grilled on every side using Cyclonic Grilling Technology. Ninja Foodi Grill is trying to outweigh the normal Air Fryer due to its multifunctional capacity which can bake, roast, air fry, or dehydrate. On most air fryers, you have to pull out a basket to toss and turn foods while frying; this can be awkward to hold the basket as you work. The Ninja Foodi Grill's lid opens upwards; it's very easy to access items that need to be flipped in the crisper basket.

Benefits of Using the Ninja Foodi Grill

1. The Ninja Foodi Grill is very easy to clean.

Cleaning the unit is not as difficult as you may think. The nonstick ceramic-coated grill grate, crisper basket, and cooking pot are all easy to clean and they are dishwasher safe in which you can deep the parts into water and wash it perfectly.

2. Ninja Foodi Grill cooks faster.

The unit uses high temperature of about 500°F to circulate rapid cyclonic air. This is what makes the Ninja Foodi Grill cook as fast as an outdoor grill.

3. It grills delicious meals.

Foods grilled with the Ninja Foodi Grill are crispier and more delicious than what you may have from the normal Air Fryer.

4. The Ninja Foodi Grill cooks low fat meals.

The grilling system of the Ninja Foodi Grill has a customizable protein and doneness settings which can enable you to perfectly cook food to your desired consistency and at a low fat content.

5. Ninja Foodi Grill has a dual sensor Foodi Smart Thermometer.

This helps the unit to continuously monitor temperature during the cooking process. All cooking process is done at a given temperature.

6. Ninja Foodi Grill is smoke free.

The Ninja Foodi Grill was manufactured to work perfectly without any smoke coming out from the unit. This is one of its unique features. The combination of a temperature-controlled grill grate, splatter shield, and cool-air zone reduces smoke.

7. Ninja Foodi grills food faster and healthy.

With Ninja Foodi Grill, you can cook your favorite foods within some few minutes even without putting any oil.

8. Ninja Foodi does not require you to flip the food over unlike Air Fryer.

This mean you can confidently grill food like fish without waiting to turn over to the other side. Superheated airflow surrounds your food so you don't need to flip foods over like burgers. no sticking, no more falling apart. This is one of its unique features of the Ninja Foodi Grill.

9. The digital control panel on the grill is easy to read and well designed.

The Ninja Foodi Grill control panel is very easy to be understood. The unit needs to be preheated first before cooking for a better result. Preheating the unit can take up to 8 minutes.

10. Ninja Foodi Grill parts are dishwasher safe.

In the top of the lid, there's a splatter shield that needs to be cleaned after each use. Luckily, all of the removable parts (including the shield) can go in the dishwasher. The interior and exterior of the machine don't get particularly dirty, thus making cleaning easy with less stress.

Accessories that Come with the Ninja Foodi Grill

1. The Ninja Foodi Grill Unit.

This part is responsible for cooking food at a very high temperature. To turn on, hit the power button on the front display and then select a cook function (grills, air crisp, dehydrate, roast or bake).

2. The Hood.

This always opens up to reveal the interior where different cooking accessories can be inserted. A splatter guard on the underside protects the heating element from grease. Cleaning it is very easy. Just make sure you have enough clearance to open the hood.

3. Cooking Pot.

The Ninja Foodi Grill pot is unique and dishwasher safe. The shape is like a deep roasting pan and it is inserted first into the Ninja Foodi Grill. It is used to hold drippings when grilling or air frying. However, the pot can also be used to roast or bake foods. Alternatively, you can even put a cake or pie pan inside to bake up a lovely dessert.

4. Grill grate.

This is another unique feature. It is dishwasher safe. It is inserted over the cooking pot for grilling and is part of the magic that helps the Ninja Foodi Grill superbly carry out those amazing grill marks. It has 2 handles on the side which allows for easy insert and removal. It is very easy to clean with some warm soapy dishwater and a scrub brush for sticky bits.

5. Crisper Basket.

The crisper basket is dishwasher Safe and is used whenever you want to air fry or dehydrate. However, the grill grate gets removed and the basket gets placed inside the cooking pot. It is very easy to remove and clean.

6. Kebab Skewers.

This makes cooking in the Ninja Foodi Grill fun. 5 skewers came packed inside the box for instant grilling fun. It is dishwasher safe and easy to clean.

7. Cleaning Brush.

This small cleaning brush is used to scrub and scrape crusted on bits left stuck to the grate and splatter shield after grilling. It is dishwasher safe and easy to clean.

Ninja Foodi Grill Functional Buttons

1. Grilling.

This is a unique and frequently used button. In order to test the grilling function, you can cook both fresh and frozen hamburgers, chicken breasts, salmon, and New York strip steaks and you will be very impressed at the result. The chicken and burgers will look like they were cooked on an outdoor grill. Even without flipping over the fish to the other side, the skin on the salmon will be delightfully crisp and the top well browned. Steaks cooked in the Ninja Foodi Grill will come out better than many steaks broiled in an oven. One of the exiting aspects of grilling is that the Ninja Foodi Grill is entirely smokeless throughout the cooking cycle.

2. Air Frying.

Air frying food in the Air Fryer and Ninja Foodi Grill, the Ninja Foodi Grill rivals the best Air Fryers. Both fresh and frozen fries came out close to those fast-food ones that you find so irresistible. Cooking in most Air Fryers require you to pull out a basket to toss and turn foods halfway to cooking cycle and it can be awkward to hold the basket as you work. But as the Ninja Foodi Grill's lid opens upwards, it's very easy to access items that need to be flipped in the crisper basket.

3. Roasting.

If you dislike turning on your oven, you can roast a small portion of meat on the Ninja Foodi Grill. A pork loin roast can be roasted tender and juicy with a crackling crust.

4. Baking.

With the Ninja Foodi Grill, you can bake a cake because the cooking pot is large enough to hold an 8-inch pan. However, a yellow cake can be evenly browned with a moist tender crumb. The Ninja Foodi Grill could be a quick way to get a homemade dessert on your table.

5. Dehydrating.

The Dehydrating button is a very unique button which also helps to cook delicious food like apple rings. However, you can only fit about 18 slices onto the Foodi at a time which can yield about a cup and a half of dried apple rings. If you like making your own dried fruits, even in small portions and you are also willing to leave the unit operating overnight, you'll be happy using the Dehydrating button and it will give you a nice result.

Steps to Use Your Ninja Foodi Grill

The Ninja Foodi Grill requires that you preheat the unit. Preheating the unit can take up to 8 minutes. For instance, if you wanted to cook boneless NY Strip steaks, ensure you use oil preferably peanut oil in order to enhance searing. The type of oil you use matters because it needs to have a high smoking point.

The next thing to do is to brush a light coating of generic vegetable oil and sprinkle on some Montreal Steak Seasoning. Set Grill Control on High temperature and allow the Ninja Foodi Grill to preheat for 8 minutes, you may add extra 8 minutes because the timer will start counting when the grill has preheated.

When the unit beeps to indicate that it has been preheated, an "Add Food" message is displayed on the control panel when the grill has preheated. You can now open the hood and place the steak on the Ninja Foodi Grill grate. Lock the hood and select Air Crisp. Grill for 8 minutes. The steak is ready to be served.

Useful Tips for Using your Ninja Foodi Grill

The Ninja Foodi Grill is very easy to be understood on how to use the appliance. The Air Crisp button works equivalent to a dedicated Air Fryer. In order to grill, you may add a small amount of oil, select Air Crisp mode and set the required temperature as long as the cooking time. You can begin the cooking process. Note, using the Air Crisp mode will not take you much time to properly cook the food but it will give you the optimum result you needed.

If the food you want to cook is more than what the Ninja Foodi Grill can contain in a single batch, you need to divide it and cook in two or three batches as the case may be. If you are cooking in batches, it's advisable you allow the unit to run for about 3 minutes between batches in order to reheat the grill grate. The oil is important because it will aid in less smoke. It is recommended that you use oil with a high smoke point example canola, coconut, avocado, vegetables, or grape seed oil. Olive oil can cause the unit to bring out smoke. While you are cooking in batches, ensure not to overcrowd the food in the Ninja Foodi Grill grate or pot. Evenly arrange and space out ingredients in a single layer to ensure consistent browning and even charring.

You also need to monitor the food to ensure they don't get burnt due to the fact that the unit cooks food at a faster rate and at a high temperature. Note, the internal temperature keeps increasing as the food rest so you need to monitor the doneness with a food Thermometer.

When air fry crisping, check food and frequently shake crisper basket for a nice result. For a nice crispiness, use recommended oil for optimum results with fresh vegetable.

Ninja Foodi Grill Troubleshooting

1. "E" pops up on the control panel display.

When you see this, there's a problem somewhere. The unit is not functioning properly. Please contact Customer Service on 1-877-646-5288 the best assistance. Please register your product online at registeryourninja.com and have the product on hand when you call.

2. "Add Pot" appears on the control panel display. This means that the pot is not properly installed in the unit.

3. "Plug In" appears on the control panel display.

This is caused by temperature probe. It needs to be plugged into the socket on the right side of the control panel. Before proceeding to cooking, ensure that it is plugged in the appropriate side.

4. "Shut Lid" appears on the control panel display.

This may happen even when the unit has completed its Grill preheating and it is time to add your ingredients.• "Shut Lid" appears on the control panel display. If this happens, it means the hood is opened and needs to be closed for the selected function to start.

5. Blinking lights appear after I press the START/STOP button. The blinking light is a progress bar indicating the preheating cycle.6. The preheating progress bar does not start from the beginning.

Note that from your previous use, when the unit is still warm, it will not require the full Preheat time.

7. Can I cancel or override preheating?

The answer is yes. You have to know that preheat is highly recommended for best results. However, you can skip preheating process by selecting the function again after you press the START/STOP button. If are using the grill function, you cannot override preheating process.

Ninja Foodi Grill Frequently Asked Questions

1. Is the Ninja Foodi Grill easy to use and clean?

The answer is yes. The control panel on the grill is well designed and easy to understand. The Ninja Foodi Grill preheats automatically and the preheat time can be over 8 minutes. In the top of the lid, it has a splatter shield that needs to be removed after each use and cleaned. All of the removable parts are dishwasher safe. The interior and exterior part of the unit is very easy to clean.

2. Should I add my ingredients before or after preheating?

The best thing to do is to preheat the unit right before adding the Ingredients.

3. My unit is emitting smoke. Why?

Please always use the recommended oil if you are using oil. Wrong oil can make the unit to smoke. If you are using the Grill function, ensure you select the recommended temperature setting. You can see the recommended settings in the Quick Start Guide and in the Inspiration guide. You also have to ensure the splatter shield is installed properly.

4. How can I pause the unit to enable me check my food?

The unit automatically pauses when the hood is opened during cooking process. If you want to pause the unit and check for proper doneness, what you need to do is to open the hood.

5. If I put the cooking pot on my countertop, is it safe?

If you do this, the pot will heat during cooking. Use caution when handling, and place on heat-safe surfaces only.

6. Why did the unit burn my food?

It is recommended that you put food into the unit when it has beeped to indicate it has been preheated. Always check the progress throughout cooking, and remove food when desired consistency has been achieved. To avoid burning, remove the food immediately the cooking cycle is completed.

7. My food didn't cook when I was using the air crisping mode.

Evenly arrange the ingredients in a layer on the bottom of the crisper basket with no overlapping. Ensure to shake loose ingredients while cooking for consistent crispiness.

8. Why is my food blowing around when I'm using air crisping mode?

You need to secure the loose food with toothpicks in order to avoid fan from blowing the lightweight foods around.

9. Can I Air Crisp fresh battered ingredients in the appliance?

The answer is yes. However, you need to use the proper breading technique. If you have flour, egg and bread crumbs to coat a particular ingredient, it is important to coat foods first with flour, egg, and then with bread crumbs respectively. Ensure to press the bread crumbs onto the food so they stick in place.

10. What can the Ninja Foodi Grill do?

As the name implies, the Ninja Foodi Grill can grill. It cooks food with the hood closed. Although the hood is closed while cooking, it doesn't press food down but it can only brand grill marks on one side at a time. The marks from the grill grate are curve not straight lines on the food. In the other hand, the Ninja Food Grill can also air fry, roast, bake, and dehydrate.

BREAKFAST RECIPES

Sweet Potato Wedges

Preparation time: 10 minutes

Cooking time: 25 minutes

Overall time: 35 minutes

Serves: 2 to 4 people

Recipe Ingredients:

- 2 sweet potatoes or yams (approx. 1 pound each)
- 1 tbsp. of canola oil
- 1 tbsp. of honey, plus more for garnish
- 1 tsp. of smoked paprika, plus more for garnish
- 1 tsp. of coarse kosher salt
- ½ tsp. of ground black pepper
- Dipping sauce of choice

Cooking Instructions:

1. Rinse and scrub sweet potatoes or yams well in cold water, then pat extremely dry.

2. Cut each in half lengthwise, then cut each half into 4 or 5 wedges. In a large bowl, mix remaining ingredients, then toss potato wedges to coat.

3. Insert crisper basket in unit. Select Air Fry, set temperature to 390°F, and set time to 24 minutes. Select the Start/Stop button to begin preheating.

4. When the unit beeps to signify it has preheated, spread wedges out evenly in basket, then close hood and cook for about 10 minutes.

5. After 10 minutes, toss or stir wedges with rubber-tipped tongs. Close hood to resume cooking for 10 more minutes.

6. After 10 minutes, check wedges for doneness. If desired, cook up to 4 more minutes until wedges achieve your desired level of crispiness.

7. When cooking is complete, toss wedges with additional honey and paprika, if desired, and serve with dipping sauce of choice.

Loaded Baked Potatoes

Preparation time: 15 minutes

Cooking time: 50 minutes

Overall time: 1 hour 5 minutes

Serves: 4 to 6 people

Recipe Ingredients:

- 5 russet of potatoes (6–8 ounces each), pierced with a fork 3 times
- 5 tsp. of unsalted butter, divided
- 1 2/3 cups of shredded cheddar cheese, divided
- 1 ¼ cup of sour cream
- 7 slices of cooked bacon, chopped
- 1 bunch of fresh scallions, chopped

Cooking Instructions:

1. Remove the crisper basket and grill grate from the pot. Select Bake, set temperature to 390°F, and set time to 40 minutes.

2. Select the Start/Pause button to begin preheating. When the unit beeps to signify it has preheated, place potatoes in pot.

3. Close hood and cook for 40 minutes. After 40 minutes, remove potatoes from grill and allow to cool for about 5 minutes.

4. After 5 minutes, make a 3-inch cut lengthwise in each potato. Press ends of potatoes toward one another to make an opening.

5. Add 1 teaspoon butter and 1/3 cup cheese to each potato. Close hood. Select Bake, set temperature to 375°F, and set time to 8 minutes.

6. Press Start/Stop to begin preheating. When the unit beeps to signify it has preheated, place potatoes in pot and cook for about 8 minutes.

7. After 8 minutes, remove potatoes and top each with 1/4 cup sour cream and one tablespoon chopped bacon. Garnish with scallions and serve immediately.

Grilled Pizza

Preparation time: 5 minutes

Cooking time: 10 minutes

Overall time: 15 minutes

Serves: 1 to 3 people

Recipe Ingredients:

- 2 tbsp. of all-purpose flour, plus more as needed
- 1 pizza dough (6 ounces)
- 1 tbsp. of canola oil, divided
- ½ cup of pizza or alfredo sauce
- 1 cup of shredded mozzarella cheese
- ½ cup of ricotta cheese
- 15 pepperoni slices, optional
- Dried oregano for serving, optional

Cooking Instructions:

1. Insert grill grate in unit and close hood. Select Grill, set temperature to MAX mode, and set time to 7 minutes.

2. Select the Start/Stop button to begin preheating. While unit is preheating, spread flour out evenly over a clean work surface.

3. Use a rolling pin to roll out the dough on the floured surface to an even thinness, adding additional flour as needed to ensure dough does not stick to rolling pin.

4. Dough should not be rolled out larger than 9 inches across, so it will fit on the grill grate.

5. Brush the surface of the rolled-out dough evenly with ½ tablespoon of canola oil. Flip dough over and brush with remaining ½ tablespoon of oil.

6. Poke dough with a fork 5 or 6 times across its surface to prevent air pockets from forming during cooking.

7. When the unit beeps to signify it has preheated, place dough on the grill grate. Close hood and cook for about 4 minutes.

8. After 4 minutes, flip dough, then spread sauce evenly over the dough. Sprinkle with cheese and pepperoni slices, if desired.

9. Close hood and continue cooking for the remaining 2 minutes, until cheese is melted and pepperoni slices begin to crisp.

10. When cooking is complete, allow to cool slightly and top with dried oregano, if desired, before slicing.

Grilled Tomato Salsa

Preparation time: 15 minutes

Cooking time: 10 minutes

Overall time: 25 minutes

Serves: 2 to 4 people

Recipe Ingredients:

- 5 Roma tomatoes, cut in half lengthwise
- 1 red onion, peeled, cut in quarters
- 1 jalapeño pepper, cut in half, seeds removed
- 1 tbsp. of kosher salt
- 2 tsp. of ground black pepper
- 2 tbsp. of canola oil1 bunch fresh cilantro, stems trimmed
- 3 cloves of garlic, peeled
- 2 tbsp. of ground cumin
- Juice and zest of 3 lime

Cooking Instructions:

1. In a large bowl, combine tomatoes, onion, jalapeño pepper, salt, and black pepper with canola oil.

2. Mix well to ensure vegetables are coated with oil and seasonings. Insert grill grate in unit and close hood.

3. Select the Grill function, set temperature to Max mode, and set time to 10 minutes. Select the Start/Stop button to begin preheating.

4. When the unit beeps to signify it has preheated, place vegetable mixture on the grill grate. Close hood and cook for about 5 minutes.

5. After 5 minutes, flip vegetables. Close hood and cook for the remaining 5 minutes. When cooking is complete, remove mixture from unit and allow to cool.

6. Transfer cooled mixture to a food processor. Add cilantro, garlic, cumin, and lime juice and zest. Pulse until desired consistency is reached.

7. Serve immediately, or chill in refrigerator first.

French Fries with Parmesan & Garlicky Mayo

Preparation time: 15 minutes

Cooking time: 20 minutes

Overall time: 35 minutes

Serves: 4 to 6 people

Recipe Ingredients:

- 1 lb. of frozen French fries
- ½ cup of mayonnaise
- 2 cloves of garlic, minced
- 1 tsp. of garlic powder
- ½ tsp. of kosher salt
- ¼ tsp. of ground black pepper
- Squeeze of lemon juice
- 1 tbsp. of canola oil
- ½ cup of grated Parmesan cheese
- 1 tbsp. of parsley, chopped

Cooking Instructions:

1. Insert crisper basket unit and close hood.

2. Select Air Fry, set temperature to 375°F, and set time to 22 minutes. Select Start/Stop to begin preheating.

3. When the unit beeps to signify it has preheated, add frozen fries to basket. Close hood and cook for about 10 minutes.

4. After the 10 minutes is up, shake basket of fries. Place basket back in unit and close hood to resume cooking.

5. Combine mayonnaise, garlic, garlic powder, salt, pepper, and lemon juice in a bowl. After 10 minutes, check fries for doneness.

6. Continue cooking up to 2 more minutes if necessary. When cooking is complete, first toss fries with canola oil and then with grated Parmesan and parsley.

7. Serve immediately with garlicky mayo sauce.

Twice Baked Potatoes

Preparation time: 20 minutes

Cooking time: 40 minutes

Overall time: 60 minutes

Serves: 2 to 4 people

Recipe Ingredients:

- 4 russets of potatoes
- 2 teaspoons of Avocado oil
- 1 ½ teaspoons of kosher salt
- 10 slices of bacon
- 1 cup of sour cream
- 2 tablespoons of milk you can use heavy cream or half n half as well
- 4 tablespoons of butter
- 3/4 teaspoon of kosher salt if you like salt use the 3/4 tsp
- ½ teaspoon of black pepper
- 1 cup of mild cheddar cheese shredded
- ¾ cups of mild cheddar cheese shredded

Cooking Instructions:

1. Place ceramic bowl and air Fry basket into Ninja Foodi grill and place the 10 slices of bacon Inuit basket, close lid.

2. Turn on Ninja Foodi grill and select air Fry, temperature. 390°F, for about 20 minutes. air crisp bacon turning a few times until desired crispiness.

3. When bacon done remove to a paper towel lined plate. Remove bowl-being careful as it is very hot. Either save bacon grease or discard the bacon fat.

4. Clean and wipe bowl and air crisp basket and place back into Ninja Foodi grill. Take a fork and poke potatoes all over.

5. Place potatoes in a wide bowl and either spray or pour avocado oil over potatoes and rub oil to cover entire potato. Liberally apply kosher salt to potatoes.

6. Clean and wash potatoes, let them dry. Place ceramic bowl into Ninja Foodi grill and the add air crisp basket as well.

7. Place the 4 potatoes into air crisp basket, close the lid. Turn Ninja Foodi grill on and select air Fry, temperature 375°F, time 45 minutes and press the start button.

8. Check potatoes in 35 minutes. Check potatoes for doneness at 35 minutes. When potatoes tests done, remove from Ninja Foodi grill.

9. Set on a bakers rack to cool for about 10 minutes or until you can handle them as they will be very hot. When potatoes are cool. Cut off the top ¼ of potato.

10. Select the bowed side of potato to remove. Reserve the tops for potato skins. After removing tops of potatoes.

11. scoop out inside of potato into a medium size bowl- and leave ¼ inch around the sides and bottom of potato-this will provide structure to the potatoes.

12. Take a potato masher or hand mixer and mash potatoes just a little to break up the inside of the potatoes.

13. Then add butter, salt, pepper, sour cream, ¾ of the cooked. bacon, ¾ of the green onions ,1 cup of cheese and start with 1 tablespoon of cream/milk.

14. Stir with a spatula to combine these ingredients. Then use a potato masher or. use hand mixer to mix all the ingredients.

15. Using a hand mixer will give you a smoother filling. If mixture too thick you can add more cream.

16. Fill the hollowed out potatoes with the filling mixture. I use a spoon and be sure to overstuff the potatoes-go high as when the potatoes cook the filling will settle.

17. When done filling the potatoes. Place in air crisp basket, select air Fry, temperature 350°F, for about 15 minutes.

18. Air crisped these for about 10 minutes and then added remaining cheese to top of stuffed potatoes and air crisp for a few more minutes until the cheese is melted.

19. When cheese is melted remove from air crisp basket onto a plate and garnish with the remaining bacon and green onion. Enjoy!

Grilled Harissa Halloumi

Preparation time: 5 minutes

Cooking time: 5 minutes

Overall time: 10 minutes

Serves: 2 to 4 people

Recipe Ingredients:

- 4 tablespoons of Harissa
- 2 teaspoons of zaatar
- 2 tablespoons of olive oil
- 450g of halloumi (2 x 225g blocks)

Cooking Instructions:

1. Insert the grill plate into the cooking pot of the unit and close the lid. Select Grill and the Max settings, and set the time for about 4 minutes.

2. Stir together the harissa paste, zaatar, and olive oil to combine. Drain the halloumi and pat dry with kitchen towel.

3. Cut each block of halloumi into 8 then toss the halloumi in the harissa paste mixture until evenly coated.

4. Once the unit has finished pre-heating and the 'Add Food' prompt comes up on the screen, place the halloumi onto the grill then close the lid.

5. Flip after 2 minutes of cooking using silicone tongs. Serve immediately with salad, in a wrap or pitta, or even a sandwich!

Grilled Citrusy Halibut

Preparation time: 10 minutes

Cooking time: 12 minutes

Overall time: 22 minutes

Serves: 1 to 3 people

Recipe Ingredients:

- Zest and juice of 1 orange
- Zest and juice of 1 lime
- 1 tsp. of ginger, minced
- 1 tsp. of garlic, minced
- 1 tsp. of kosher salt
- 1 tsp. of ground black pepper
- 2 tbsp. of canola oil
- 1 tbsp. of parsley, minced
- 2 tbsp. of honey
- 2 frozen halibut fillets (6 ounces each)

Cooking Instructions:

1. Insert grill grate in unit and close hood. Select Grill mode, set temperature to Max, and set time to 12 minutes.

2. Select Start/Stop to begin preheating. While unit is preheating, combine all ingredients, except halibut fillets, in a bowl and mix well to incorporate.

3. Place fillets in the bowl and generously spoon marinade over them, coating evenly. When the unit beeps to signify it has preheated, place fillets on the grill grate.

4. Pour a spoonful of marinade over the top of each fillet, then close the hood and cook for about 10 to 12 minutes, until internal temperature reaches 140°F.

5. For an additional infusion of flavor, baste the fillets with marinade every 3 to 4 minutes. When cooking is complete, serve immediately.

Classic Cheeseburgers

Preparation time: 10 minutes

Cooking time: 10 minutes

Overall time: 20 minutes

Serves: 2 to 4 people

Recipe Ingredients:

- ½ lb. of uncooked ground beef
- 4 slices of American cheese
- (80% lean) 4 burger buns
- Kosher salt, as desired
- Ground black pepper, as desired

Toppings:

- Lettuce
- Red onion
- Tomatoes
- Pickles
- Condiments

Cooking Instructions:

1. Insert grill grate in unit and close hood. Select the Grill function, set temperature to High mode, and set time to 8 minutes for medium-cooked burgers.

2. Select Start/Stop to begin preheating. While unit is preheating, divide the ground beef into 4 portions and hand-form each into a loosely formed 4-inch patty.

3. With your thumb, make a 1-inch indent in the center of each patty, season patties with salt and pepper, as desired.

4. When the unit beeps to signify it has preheated, place patties on the grill grate, gently pressing them down to maximize grill marks.

5. Close hood and cook for about 6 minutes. When done, serve immediately and Enjoy!

Grilled Cauliflower Steaks with Greek Salsa

Preparation time: 10 minutes

Cooking time: 30 minutes

Overall time: 40 minutes

Serves: 3 to 5 people

Recipe Ingredients:

- 1 head of cauliflower, leaves and stem removed
- 1/3 cup of Kalamata olives, chopped, pits removed
- ½ cup of roasted red peppers, chopped
- 1 tbsp. of fresh oregano, minced
- 1 tbsp. of fresh parsley, minced
- 3 cloves of garlic, peeled, minced
- Juice of 1 lemon
- ½ lb. (8 oz.) of feta cheese, crumbled
- Kosher salt, as desired
- 1 tsp. of ground black pepper
- 1/3 cup walnuts, roughly chopped
- 1 small red onion, peeled, chopped
- ¼ cup of canola oil, divided

Cooking Instructions:

1. Cut cauliflower from top to bottom into two 2-inch "steaks"; reserve remaining cauliflower.

2. In a large bowl, stir together olives, roasted red peppers, oregano, parsley, garlic, lemon juice, feta, salt, pepper, walnuts, red onion, and 2 tablespoons of canola oil.

3. Insert grill grate in unit and close hood. Select Grill function, set temperature to Max, and set time to 17 minutes.

4. Select the Start/Stop button to begin preheating. While unit is preheating, brush remaining 2 tablespoons of oil on both sides of steaks.

5. Season each with salt, as desired. When the unit beeps to signify it has preheated, place steaks on the grill grate.

6. Close hood and cook for about 10 minutes. After 10 minutes, flip steaks. Close hood and continue cooking for about 5 minutes.

7. After 5 minutes, spread "steaks" generously with Greek salsa. Close hood and cook for the remaining 2 minutes.

8. Reserve remaining Greek salsa. When cooking is complete, serve immediately.

Rice & Vegetable Stuffed Peppers

Preparation time: 15 minutes

Cooking time: 30 minutes

Overall time: 45 minutes

Serves: 2 to 4 people

Recipe Ingredients:

- 6 red or green bell peppers, top 1/2-inch sections cut off and reserved, seeds and ribs removed from the insides
- 4 cloves of garlic, minced
- Small white onion, peeled, diced
- Bags (8.5 ounces) instant rice, cooked in microwave
- 1 can (10 ounces) of red enchilada sauce
- 1 package (1 ounce) of fajita spice mix
- 1 can (4 ounces) of diced green chilis, drained
- ½ cup of vegetable stock 1 bag (8 ounces) shredded
- Colby Jack cheese, divided

Cooking Instructions:

1   Chop the ½-inch portions of reserved bell peppers and place in a large mixing bowl.

2   Add all other ingredients to mixing bowl, except whole bell peppers and half the cheese. Use cooking pot without grill grate or crisper basket installed.

3   Close the hood and select Roast function, set temperature to 350°F, and set time to 32 minutes.

4   Select the Start/Stop to begin preheating. While unit is preheating, spoon the mixture into the peppers, filling them up as fully as possible.

5   Lightly press mixture down into the peppers to fit more in. When the unit beeps to signify it has preheated, place peppers, standing upright, in the pot.

6   Close hood and cook for about 30 minutes. After 30 minutes, evenly sprinkle remaining cheese over the top of the peppers.

7   Close hood and cook for the remaining 2 minutes. When cooking is complete, serve immediately.

Grilled Donuts

Preparation time: 5 minutes

Cooking time: 10 minutes

Overall time: 15 minutes

Serves: 6 to 8 people

Recipe Ingredients:

- 2 cups of powdered sugar
- ¼ cup of whole milk
- 1 tsp. of vanilla extract
- 1 tube (16 ounces) of prepared biscuit dough
- Cooking spray
- Rainbow or chocolate sprinkles, as desired
- Crumbled cookies, as desired
- Cinnamon sugar, as desired
- Mini marshmallows, as desired

Cooking Instructions:

1. In a medium bowl, combine powdered sugar, milk, and vanilla extract.

2. Whisk well to create a sugar glaze and set aside. Lay biscuit dough on a cutting board or a clean, flat work surface.

3. Using a 1-inch ring mold, cut a hole in the center of each round of dough. Place dough rounds on a plate and refrigerate for about 5 minutes.

4. Install grill grate in unit and close hood. Select Grill, set temperature to Medium, and set time to 6 minutes.

5. Select Start/Stop to begin preheating. After 5 minutes, remove dough rounds from refrigerator and coat with cooking spray on both sides.

6. When the unit beeps to signify it has preheated, place 4 dough rounds on grill grate. Close hood and cook for about 3 minutes.

7. After 3 minutes, remove donuts from unit using rubber-tipped tongs. Place remaining 4 dough rounds on grill grate, then close hood and cook for 3 minutes.

8. When cooking is complete, remove donuts from unit using rubber-tipped tongs. Let donuts cool for about 5 minutes.

9. When donuts are cool enough to handle, dunk one side of each in the sugar glaze, being sure to coat liberally and evenly.

10. Place donuts on a plate, glaze-side up, and sprinkle with toppings as desired. Serve immediately.

Rose and Honey Grilled Fruits with Baklava Crunch

Preparation time: 10 minutes

Cooking time: 15 minutes

Overall time: 25 minutes

Serves: 2 to 4 people

Recipe Ingredients:

- Baklava crunch
- 70g of gluten-free oats
- 25g of coconut sugar
- 25g of walnuts
- 2 teaspoons of ground cinnamon
- 1 teaspoon of ground cardamom (seeds from 12 pods)
- ½ teaspoon of ground ginger
- 1/8 teaspoon of cloves
- Pinch sea salt
- 35g of butter (cubed)
- Grilled Fruit
- 1 tablespoon of honey
- 1 tablespoon of water
- 1 teaspoon rose water
- Zest ½ orange
- 2 peaches (halved, de-stoned)
- 2 plums (halved, de-stoned)
- Yogurt Sauce
- 150g of Greek yogurt
- Remaining glaze from grilled fruit

Cooking Instructions:

1. Place the Crisper Pan into the cooking pot. Select Air Fry, set temperature to 150°C and time to 5 minutes. Select Start/Stop to begin pre-heating.

2. Whilst the unit is pre-heating, combine dry ingredients for the baklava crunch then add the butter. Rub together until mixture resembles bread crumbs.

3. Once the unit has pre-heated add the baklava crunch mix to the Crisper Pan and spread out with the back of a spoon.

4. Close lid and cook until halfway mark. Open and give the mixture a stir then resume cooking.

5. Combine the honey, water, rose water, and orange zest into a small bowl to create a glaze.

6. When the unit has completed cooking remove the cooking pot, then lift out crisper pan and leave to cool.

7. Place the cooking pot back into the unit, insert grill plate, and close lid. Select the Grill function, set temperature to Max mode and time to 6 minutes.

8. Select Start/Stop to begin pre-heating. When the unit beeps and displays 'Add Food' prompt, glaze the flat side of the fruits.

9. Place face down onto the grill plate. Glaze the tops then close the lid. Halfway through cooking glaze tops again then flip and glaze the underside.

10. Close lid until cooking is complete. After the final glaze combine the Greek yogurt and remaining glaze mixture and set to one side.

11. Once finished cooking, serve fruit immediately with the baklava crunch and yogurt sauce.

Pesto & Goat's Cheese Flatbread

Preparation time: 5 minutes

Cooking time: 15 minutes

Overall time: 20 minutes

Serves: 2 to 4 people

Recipe Ingredients:

- Ready to use pizza dough
- Freshly chopped fresh basil
- 3 tbsp. of pesto
- 40g of goat's cheese, crumbled
- 30g of Parmesan, finely grated
- 30g of sun-dried tomatoes
- Olive oil for brushing and drizzling
- Salt & freshly ground black pepper

Cooking Instructions:

1. Insert grill plate in unit and close lid. Select Grill, set temperature to High and set time to 2 minutes.

2. Select Start/Stop to begin preheating and roll out pizza dough and pierce lightly with a fork to prevent too many air bubbles.

3. When the unit beeps to signify it has pre-heated, place rolled out dough on top of grill plate, close the lid and allow to cook for about 2 minutes.

4. Once there is 1-minute left on the timer flip the dough. When the cooking process has finished remove the flatbread from the unit and set to the side.

5. Leave the grill plate in unit, select Grill, set temperature to High mode and set time to 4 minutes. Select Start/Stop to begin preheating.

6. Lightly brush edges of flatbread with olive oil. Spread the pesto evenly on the flatbread leaving about 1 cm around the edges.

7. Then sprinkle with goat's cheese and parmesan. When unit beeps to signify it has preheated, open lid and place flatbread on the grill plate.

8. Close lid and allow to cook. Once unit beeps to signify the cooking process has finished, remove flatbread from the unit.

9. Place on a cutting board and dress with dried tomatoes, freshly cut basil and freshly grounded salt and pepper.

10. Lightly drizzle with olive oil and serve immediately.

CHICKEN AND POULTRY RECIPE
Chicken Couscous Bowl

Preparation time: 5 minutes

Cooking time: 20 minutes

Overall time: 25 minutes

Serves: 1 to 3 people

Recipe Ingredients:

- 120ml of water
- 1 tablespoon of Siracha sauce
- ½ vegetable stock cube
- 120g of couscous
- 2 chicken breasts, sliced
- 1 tablespoon of oil
- 1 teaspoon of paprika
- 1 teaspoon of garlic powder
- Salt & pepper
- 1 bell pepper, deseeded and diced
- 1 onion, peeled and diced
- 2 tomatoes, diced
- 2 tablespoons of tomato puree
- Feta cheese and parsley for garnish

Cooking Instructions:

1. Boil 120 ml water and add vegetable stock to it. Stir until stock is dissolved.

2. Place couscous in a bowl and pour vegetable stock over it. Cover the bowl and set to the side.

3. Ensure pot is installed but grill plate is removed. Select Roast, set temperature to 200°C and set timer to 15 minutes.

4. Select Start/Stop to begin preheating. In a bowl combine chicken, oil, paprika, garlic powder, salt and pepper.

5. Once unit has beeped to signify it has preheated add the seasoned chicken and close lid to begin cooking.

6. When 10 minutes are left on the timer, open lid and add bell pepper, onion and tomatoes. Close lid to continue cooking.

7. When 3 minutes are left on the timer add Siracha, tomato puree and already cooked couscous and stir well.

8. Once cooking process has completed stir in parsley and garnish with feta cheese. Serve hot.

Peri Peri Grilled Chicken

Preparation time: 10 minutes

Cooking time: 20 minutes

Overall time: 30 minutes

Serves: 2 to 4 people

Recipe Ingredients:

For the chicken:

- 4 whole chicken legs, skin on

For the marinade:

- Juice of ½ a lemon or lime (or 50 ml bottled)
- 3 crushed garlic cloves (optional)

For the Peri Peri sauce:

- ¼ red pepper or 1- 2 fiery red chillies
- ½ tsp cayenne pepper
- 2 cloves of garlic
- 50ml of lemon or lime juice
- 2 teaspoons of smoked paprika
- 50mls of olive oil

For the garlic bread:

- 2 French baguettes
- 4 tablespoons of olive oil (more if you need)
- 2 crushed garlic cloves
- 2 crushed garlic cloves
- Pinch of salt

Cooking Instructions:

1. To prepare the marinade mix the garlic, lime and salt together and pour over the chicken. Cover and leave to marinade for an hour.

2. Insert grill plate into your Ninja Foodi Grill and close the lid. Turn the grill function to high and set the timer for about 30 minutes.

3. Hit the start button. Once the Ninja beeps, it means it's a perfect temperature. Sprinkle the chicken with a little salt.

4. Put it skin side down onto the grill, closing the lid. Take a look after ten minutes, and if the skin looks nicely sizzled with grill marks.

5. turn it over, close the lid and cook for another ten minutes. Then brush both sides with the Peri Peri sauce and cook for another 5 minutes, turn over halfway through.

6. Take a piece of chicken out and with the point of a sharp knife prick into the chicken near the joint to check if it's cooked through.

7. Then let it rest on a warmed plate whilst you make the garlic bread. Set the grill on medium for 6 minutes and mix the olive oil, oregano and garlic together.

8. Cut the bread lengthways and then dip into the herbed, garlic oil. Place on the Grill and cook for about 3 to 5 minutes.

9. Serve immediately and Enjoy!

Curry Chicken Skewers with Mint Dip

Preparation time: 15 minutes

Cooking time 1 hour

Overall time: 1 hour 15 minutes

Serves: 2 to 4 people

Recipe Ingredients:

- 4 chicken breasts – cut into 2x2cm cubes
- 1 tbsp. of tomato puree
- 1 tbsp. of rapeseed oil
- ¼ tbsp. of garlic powder
- ¼ tsp. of turmeric
- ¼ tsp. of garam masala
- ¼ tsp. of ginger powder
- 1 tsp. of chili powder
- Salt and pepper
- Mint Dip
- 150g of plain yoghurt
- ½ cucumber – grated
- 10 mint leaves – finely chopped
- 1 tbsp. of lemon juice
- Salt and pepper
- Coriander leaves for garnish

Cooking Instructions:

1. In a bowl combine chicken with tomato puree, oil and all spices and set it to the side and let it marinate for 1 hour.

2. Combine grated cucumber with yoghurt, mint, lemon juice, salt and pepper and refrigerate until serving.

3. Insert grill plate in the unit and close lid. Select Grill, set temperature to Max and set time to 10 minutes.

4. Select Start/Stop to begin preheating. While unit is preheating, assemble the skewers until they're almost full.

5. When the unit beeps to signify it has preheated, place skewers on the grill plate. Close lid and cook for about 5 minutes.

6. After 5 minutes, flip the skewers and continue cooking. When cooking is complete, serve hot with mint dip.

Juicy Grilled Chicken Breasts

Preparation time: 10 minutes

Cooking time: 25 minutes

Overall time: 35 minutes

Serves: 3 to 5 people

Recipe Ingredients:

- 4 chicken breasts
- 1/3 cup of olive oil
- 3 tablespoons of soy sauce
- 2 tablespoons of balsamic vinegar
- ¼ cup of brown sugar
- 1 tablespoon of Worcestershire sauce
- 3 teaspoons of minced garlic
- Salt & pepper to taste

Cooking Instructions:

1. In a bowl mix together oil, soy sauce, balsamic vinegar, brown sugar, Worcestershire, garlic & salt & pepper.

2. Set aside ¼ cup for using later when serving. If you breasts are super thick and or uneven in thickness, put between saran wrap and beat until even and less thick.

3. Poke breasts with a fork creating little pockets for the marinade to soak into. Put your breasts into the marinade and let marinade for at least 20 minutes.

4. Insert removable cooking pot. Insert grill grate into your pot. Press grill button, set temperature to Medium, set time to 25 minutes.

5. Once Add Food flashes, add chicken breasts onto grill, close lid and cook at 8 to 10 minutes, open grill and flip meat, closing grill once again.

6. Cook for another 5 minutes, open the lid and baste the chicken with more marinade. Cover and cook another 5 minutes.

7. Start to check the internal temp to make sure you are not starting to overcook. You want to have an internal temp of 165°F.

8. Flip meat one last time and baste one more time. Cook as long as needed until you reach your internal temp of 165°F.

9. Allow meat to rest 5 minutes before cutting and serving.

Grill Greek Chicken with Tzatziki sauce

Preparation time: 10 minutes

Cooking time: 15 minutes

Overall time: 25 minutes

Serves: 2 to 4 people

Recipe Ingredients:

For the grilled chicken breasts:

- 4 chicken breasts
- ¼ cup of extra-virgin olive oil
- 2 tsp. of dried oregano
- 1 tsp. of garlic powder
- Juice of one medium lemon
- Sea salt and freshly cracked pepper to taste

For the tzatziki sauce:

- ½ cup of finely grated cucumber
- 1 cup of Greek yogurt (or sour cream)
- 2 teaspoons of apple cider vinegar
- Juice of one medium lemon
- 1 tbsp. of garlic powder (or 1-2 minced garlic cloves)

Cooking Instructions:

1. Whisk together the lemon juice, olive oil, oregano, salt, pepper, and garlic powder in a medium bowl.

2. Pour into a Ziploc bag or container with the chicken to marinate in the refrigerator for at least 2 hours.

3. Meanwhile, make the tzatziki sauce by first grating the cucumbers. Add in the Greek yogurt, vinegar, garlic, lemon juice, and sea salt to taste in a bowl.

4. Chill in the refrigerator until ready to serve. Heat up your Ninja Foodi grill to 400°F.

5. Add the marinated chicken and cook the chicken breasts for about 5 to 7 minutes per side, depending on thickness.

6. Remove from grill and allow the cooked chicken to rest. To serve, plate sliced chicken over a bed of rice or stuffed into a pita.

7. Top with the creamy tzatziki sauce and a lemon wedge. Enjoy!

Brined & Grilled Chicken Legs with Stir-Fried Vegetables

Preparation time: 10 minutes

Cooking time: 20 minutes

Overall time: 30 minutes

Serves: 1 to 3 people

Recipe Ingredients:

- 2 cups of hot water
- 2 tbsp. of kosher salt, plus more as desired
- 1 tbsp. of honey
- 2 cloves of garlic, peeled, smashed
- 4 sprigs of fresh thyme
- Juice of 1 lemon
- 2 cups of cold water
- 2 bone-in, skin-on chicken legs (drumsticks and thighs)
- 2 tbsp. of canola oil, divided
- Ground black pepper as desired
- 1 cup of Yukon potato, diced
- ½ cup of red onion, diced
- 6 baby bella mushrooms, rinsed, stems removed

Cooking Instructions:

1. In a bowl, combine hot water, 2 tablespoons of salt, honey, garlic, thyme, and lemon juice, stirring well until salt and honey have completely dissolved.

2. Then add cold water, stir to combine, and refrigerate up to 30 minutes until brine is cooled.

3. Place chicken in a medium-sized resealable plastic bag, then pour cooled brine over chicken.

4. Seal bag tightly, then place in refrigerator for a minimum of 2 hours and up to 6 hours.

5. Insert grill grate in unit. Place the Ninja Veggie Tray on grill grate and close hood. Select Grill, set temperature to High mode, and set time to 22 minutes.

6. Select Start/Stop to begin preheating. While unit is preheating, remove chicken from brine and pat dry.

7. Brush all sides of chicken with 1 tablespoon oil, then season with salt and pepper, as desired.

8. In a bowl, toss potatoes with ½ tablespoon of oil and season with salt and pepper, as desired.

9. Once the unit has beeped to signify it has preheated, place chicken skin-side down on the grill grate. Place potatoes on tray, close the hood and cook for 10 minutes.

10. Meanwhile, in a bowl, toss onion and mushrooms with remaining ½ tablespoon of oil and season with kosher salt and pepper, as desired.

11. After 10 minutes, open hood and flip chicken using rubber-tipped tongs. Stir potatoes with a rubber-tipped spatula.

12. Add onion and mushrooms on top of potatoes. Close hood to continue cooking for about 8 minutes. After 8 minutes, open hood and check chicken for doneness.

13. If necessary, cook chicken up to 4 more minutes, or until centermost part of chicken reads at least 165°F on a digital food thermometer.

14. When cooking is complete, remove chicken and vegetables from grill and serve.

Lemon and Herb Chicken Skewers

Preparation time: 10 minutes

Cooking time: 40 minutes

Overall time: 50 minutes

Serves: 4 to 6 people

Recipe Ingredients:

- 2 pounds of chicken breast cut into 1-inch chunks
- 3 teaspoons of garlic powder
- 1 teaspoon of onion powder
- ½ teaspoon of chilli powder
- 1 teaspoon of paprika powder
- ¼ teaspoon of oregano
- ¼ teaspoon of basil
- Juice of 1 lemon and zest of 2 Lemons
- 1 teaspoon of salt
- ¼ teaspoon of black pepper
- 3 tablespoons of oil

Cooking Instructions:

1. Presoak skewers for about 30 minutes. Mix together all of the ingredients apart from the chicken to make a marinade.

2. marinade the chicken in this mixture for about 30 minutes. Thread the chicken onto the skewers.

3. Insert grill plate in the grill and select grill and set to medium. Set timer to 18 minutes.

4. When pre-heating is complete (and the grill beeps), add the skewers. Cook for about 20 minutes, turning and basting midway.

5. Serve immediately and Enjoy!

Tandoori Chicken

Preparation time: 5 minutes

Cooking time: 15 minutes

Overall time: 20 minutes

Serves: 4 to 6 people

Recipe Ingredients:

- 2 pounds of chicken thighs or legs
- 125g of plain yoghurt
- 1-inch of ginger, crushed
- 6 garlic cloves, crushed
- 1 tablespoon of kashmiri chilli powder
- 2 tablespoons of tandoori paste or powder
- ½ teaspoon of turmeric
- 1.5 teaspoons of coriander powder
- 1 teaspoon of cumin powder
- 1 teaspoon of garam masala
- Salt
- 1 tablespoon of lemon juice
- 2 tablespoons of ghee, oil and spray oil

Cooking Instructions:

1. Cut 2 large slits into each chicken thigh or leg.

2. In a large bowl, combine all the ingredients with the chicken and rub the marinade in. Allow the chicken to marinate for a minimum of 30 minutes but up to 24 hours.

3. Insert the grill plate in to the Ninja Foodi Grill and close the lid. Select Grill, set the temperature to the highest option and set the timer for 18 minutes.

4. Spray with oil and add the chicken to the grill plate and flip the chicken midway through cooking and baste.

5. Check that the chicken is cooked through fully before removing. Place back on the grill for a few more minutes if required. Serve with naan or rice

Cheesy Chicken Quesadilla Stacks

Preparation time: 15 minutes

Cooking time: 30 minutes

Overall time: 45 minutes

Serves: 6 to 8 people

Recipe Ingredients:

- 4 (20cm) flour tortillas
- Cooking spray
- 80g of salsa
- 80g of sour cream
- 5 drops of hot sauce
- 350g (approx) of grilled chicken breast, chopped, divided
- 5 spring of onions, chopped, divided
- 1 can (100g) of diced jalapeño peppers, divided
- 480g plus 60g grated cheddar, divided

Cooking Instructions:

1. Insert grill plate in unit and close lid. Select Grill and set temperature to MAX, and set time to 4 minutes.

2. Select Start/Stop to begin preheating. While unit is preheating, spray both sides of the tortillas with cooking spray.

3. Then use a knife to poke 5 to 7 small holes in each tortilla (to prevent them from ballooning during cooking).

4. In a small bowl, stir together salsa, sour cream, hot sauce; set aside. When the unit beeps to signify it has preheated, place 1 tortilla on the grill plate.

5. Close lid and grill for 1 minute. After 1-minute, open lid and remove tortilla and set aside. Repeat with remaining 3 tortillas.

6. Evenly spread a grilled tortilla with a third of the chopped chicken, a third of the spring onions, a third of the jalapeño peppers, 160g cheese, and a third of the salsa mixture.

7. Place another tortilla on top. Top that tortilla with a third of the chopped chicken, a third of the spring onions, a third of the jalapeño peppers, 160g cheese, and a third of the salsa mixture.

8. Place another tortilla on top. After placing the last tortilla on top, press down gently.

9. Remove grill plate from unit. Select Roast, set temperature to 180°C, and set time to 23 minutes.

10. Select Start/Stop to begin preheating. When the unit beeps to signify it has pre-heat place tortilla stack in pot.

11. Then cover it with an aluminum foil tent, pressing down gently to secure foil around stack. Close lid and cook for about 20 minutes.

12. After 20 minutes, remove foil. Sprinkle remaining cheese over the top, close lid, and cook for the remaining 3 minutes.

13. When cooking is complete, remove with a non-metal spatula and transfer to plate, slice slack and serve.

Portuguese Grilled Chicken

Preparation time: 10 minutes

Cooking time: 50 minutes

Overall time: 1 hour

Serves: 2 to 4 people

Recipe Ingredients:

- 4 whole chicken legs, skin on
- 3 tablespoons of oil
- Juice of ½ Lemon
- 3 cloves of garlic, crushed
- Salt
- Black pepper
- 4 tablespoons of peri peri sauce of choice

Cooking Instructions:

1. Marinade the chicken with oil, garlic, lemon, salt and pepper for about 30 minutes.

2. Insert grill plate into the unit and close the lid. Turn the grill function to high and set the timer for about 30 minutes.

3. Press the start button and add chicken and grill 12 minutes and turn. Cook for a further 10 minutes.

4. Brush both sides with the Peri Peri sauce and cook for another 3 – 4 minutes, turning over midway.

5. Serve immediately and Enjoy!

Honey Rosemary Chicken Wings

Preparation time: 10 minutes

Cooking time: 30 minutes

Overall time: 40 minutes

Serves: 2 to 4 people

Recipe Ingredients:

- 1 tbsp. of kosher salt
- ½ tsp. of baking powder
- 1 tsp. of paprika
- 2 lb. of chicken wings, rinsed, patted dry
- 1 tbsp. of garlic, minced
- 1 tbsp. of lemon juice
- 1 tsp. of crushed red pepper
- 1 tbsp. of fresh rosemary, chopped
- ¼ cup of honey

Cooking Instructions:

1. Insert crisper basket in unit and close hood. Select Air Fry function, set temperature to 390°F, and set time to 27 minutes.

2. Select Start/Stop to begin preheating. While unit is preheating, stir together salt, baking powder, and paprika in a large mixing bowl.

3. When the unit beeps to signify it has preheated, place wings in crisper basket, spreading out evenly.

4. Close the hood and cook for about 12 minutes. While wings are cooking, combine garlic, lemon juice, crushed red pepper, rosemary, and honey in a mixing bowl.

5. After 12 minutes, flip the wings with rubber-tipped tongs. Close hood and cook for about 12 more minutes.

6. After 12 minutes, transfer wings to the bowl with sauce and toss to coat. Then return them to the basket.

7. Reserve any leftover sauce. Continue cooking for the remaining 3 minutes. When cooking is complete, remove wings from unit and toss in the remaining sauce.

8. Serve immediately and Enjoy!

Nashville Hot Fried Chicken

Preparation time: 5 minutes

Cooking time: 20 minutes

Overall time: 25 minutes

Serves: 2 to 4 people

Recipe Ingredients:

- 2 tbsp. of garlic powder
- 2 tbsp. of onion powder
- 2 tbsp. of chili powder
- 1 tbsp. of mustard powder
- 2 tbsp. of kosher salt1 tablespoon ground black pepper
- 1 quart (4 cups) of buttermilk
- 2 uncooked bone-in, skin-on chicken thighs
- 2 uncooked bone-in, skin-on chicken breasts, each split in half
- 4 cups of all-purpose flour
- ¾ cup of canola oil, divided
- 2 tbsp. of dark brown sugar
- 3 tbsp. of paprika
- 2 tsp. of cayenne pepper

Cooking Instructions:

1. Stir together garlic, onion, chili, and mustard powders with salt and pepper. Place half the mixture in a large resealable plastic bag or container.

2. Add buttermilk to bag or container and combine with spice mixture and set aside remaining spice mixture.

3. Add chicken to buttermilk mixture and marinate in refrigerator for about 8 hours or overnight. Strain chicken from marinade.

4. Combine remaining spice rub with flour in a large mixing bowl. Working in batches, toss chicken pieces in spiced flour mixture until evenly coated.

5. Gently tap chicken off to remove excess flour. Rub each piece of chicken with oil, using a total of ¼ cup of oil for all pieces.

6. Plug temperature probe into unit. Insert air crisp basket in unit and close hood. Select the Air Fry functions and set temperature to 360°F.

7. Select the TEMP iQ and set temperature to 170°F. Select Start/Stop to begin preheating.

8. While unit is preheating, insert probe into the center of the largest piece of chicken close to (but not touching) the bone.

9. Once the unit beeps to signify it has preheated, place chicken in the basket. Close hood over the probe cord.

10. While chicken is cooking, whisk together remaining ¼ cup of canola oil, brown sugar, paprika, and cayenne pepper in a bowl.

11. When the internal temp reads 120°F, open hood and flip chicken. Then close hood and continue cooking until the unit beeps and the probe icon flashes to signify cooking is complete.

12. When cooking is complete, remove chicken from unit and use oven mitts to remove probe from chicken. Gently toss chicken with spiced oil mixture and serve.

Cheesy Chicken Quesadilla Stacks

Preparation time: 15 minutes

Cooking time: 30 minutes

Overall time: 45 minutes

Serves: 2 to 4 people

Recipe Ingredients:

- 4 (8-inch) flour tortillas
- Vegetable oil cooking spray
- 1/3 cup of salsa
- 1/3 cup of sour cream
- 5 dashes of hot sauce
- 12 oz. of grilled chicken breast, chopped, divided 5 scallions, chopped, divided
- 1 can (4 ounces) of diced jalapeño peppers, divided
- 2 cups (8 ounces) of scallions
- 1/4 cup shredded cheddar or Colby Jack cheese, divided

Cooking Instructions:

1. Insert grill grate in unit and close hood. Select Grill function, set temperature to MAX mode, and set time to 4 minutes.

2. Select Start/Stop to begin preheating. While unit is preheating, spray both sides of the tortillas with cooking spray.

3. Then use a knife tip to poke 5 to 7 small holes in each tortilla. In a small bowl, stir together salsa, sour cream, hot sauce and set it aside.

4. When the unit beeps to signify it has preheated, place 1 tortilla on the grill grate. Close hood and grill for 1 minute.

5. After 1 minute, open hood and remove tortilla; set aside. Repeat with remaining 3 tortillas.

6. Evenly spread a grilled tortilla with a third of the chopped chicken, a third of the scallions, a third of the jalapeño peppers, 2/3 cup cheese, and a third of the salsa mixture.

7. Place another tortilla on top. Top that tortilla with a third of the chopped chicken, a third of the scallions, a third of the jalapeño peppers, 2/3 cup cheese, and a third of the salsa mixture.

8. Place another tortilla on top. After placing the last tortilla on top, press down gently. Remove grill grate from unit.

9. Select Roast, set temperature to 350°F, and set time to 23 minutes. Select Start/Stop to begin preheating.

10. When the unit beeps to signify it has preheated, place tortilla stack in pot. Then cover it with an aluminum foil tent.

11. Press down gently to secure foil around stack. Close hood and cook for about 20 minutes.

12. After 20 minutes, remove foil. Sprinkle remaining ¼ cup of cheese over the top, close hood, and cook for the remaining 3 minutes.

13. When cooking is complete, remove with a non-metal spatula and transfer to plate, slice slack and serve

Mustard-Rubbed Half Chicken

Preparation time: 10 minutes

Cooking time: 35 minutes

Overall time: 45 minutes

Serves: 2 to 4 people

Recipe Ingredients:

- ¼ cup of Dijon mustard
- ¼ cup of canola oil1 tablespoon kosher salt
- 1 tsp. of ground black pepper
- 2 tbsp. of honey
- 1 tbsp. of dry oregano
- 2 tsp. of dry Italian seasoning
- 1 tbsp. of lemon juice1 half chicken, approximately 24 ounces

Cooking Instructions:

1. In a small bowl, mix all ingredients except chicken. Coat chicken on all sides with mustard rub.

2. Plug temperature probe into unit. Insert Ninja Roasting Rack in pot and close hood. Select Roast and set temperature to 350°F.

3. Select the TEMP iQ and set temperature to 170°F. Select Start/Stop to begin preheating.

4. While unit is preheating, insert probe into center of chicken breast. Once unit has beeped to signify it has preheated.

5. Place chicken, skin-side down, on the roasting rack. Close hood over probe cord. When the display reads 140°F, open hood and flip chicken.

6. Close hood and continue cooking until the unit beeps and the probe icon flashes to signify cooking is complete.

7. Open the hood and remove chicken from grill; chicken will continue to cook even after removed from the grill.

8. Leave probe in chicken and connected to unit to monitor temperature of chicken while it rests. Allow chicken to rest up to 10 minutes before serving.

9. To check the internal temp at any time, press TEMP iQ for 2 seconds until the screen displays the internal temp.

Barbecue Chicken Breasts

Preparation: 5 minutes

Cooking time: 25 minutes

Overall time: 30 minutes

Serves: 2 to 4 people

Recipe Ingredients:

- 4 frozen boneless, skinless
- Kosher salt, as desired
- chicken breasts (8 ounces each)
- Ground black pepper, as desired
- 2 tbsp. of canola oil, divided
- 1 cup of your favorite barbecue sauce

Cooking Instructions:

1. Insert grill grate in unit and close hood. Select Grill, set temperature to Medium, and set time to 25 minutes.

2. Select Start/Stop to begin preheating. While unit is preheating, evenly brush each chicken breast with ½ tablespoon of canola oil.

3. Then season with salt and pepper, as desired. When the unit beeps to signify it has preheated, place chicken breasts on grill grate.

4. Close hood and cook for about 10 minutes. After 10 minutes, flip chicken. Close hood to continue cooking for about 5 minutes.

5. Serve immediately and Enjoy!

FISH AND SEAFOOD

Sweet and Spicy Salmon

Preparation time: 5 minutes

Cooking time: 10 minutes

Overall time: 15 minutes

Serves: 1 to 3 people

Recipe Ingredients:

- 3 salmon fillets (200g each)
- 1 tablespoon of soft light brown sugar
- 4 cloves of garlic, crushed
- 1 teaspoon of cumin powder
- ½ teaspoon of red chilli powder
- ¼ teaspoon of turmeric
- ½ tablespoon tamarind
- ½ teaspoon of salt
- 2 tablespoons of oil
- 2 tablespoons of lemon

Cooking Instructions:

1. Mix together all of the ingredients apart from the salmon to create a marinade Marinade the salmon in the mixture for about 1 hour.

2. Pre heat the Ninja Grill. Place the salmon fillets on the grill plate, set to high and close the lid.

3. Cook for about 10 to 12 minutes. Check midway and if it is grilling too fast, adjust temperature and time.

4. Serve immediately and Enjoy!

Air Grill Salmon Tacos

Preparation time: 15 minutes

Cooking time: 10 minutes

Overall time: 25 minutes

Serves: 1 to 3 people

Recipe Ingredients:

For the salmon:

- 2 pieces of salmon
- 1 clove garlic - minced
- ½ teaspoon of fresh chili pepper – finely chopped
- Lime zest
- 1 tablespoon of olive oil
- Salt and pepper to taste

For the guacamole:

- 1 avocado
- ½ small onion, finely chopped
- ½ lime juice
- ½ tomato, finely chopped
- 1 garlic clove, minced
- 1 tablespoon of coriander
- ½ tablespoon of fresh chili pepper, finely chopped
- Salt and pepper to taste
- 4 Tortillas
- Lettuce
- Tomatoes, finely chopped
- Coriander & Cheese for garnish

Cooking Instructions:

1. Mix garlic, chili pepper, lemon zest, olive oil, salt and pepper and rub on salmon and set it aside and let marinate.

2. Select Grill and set the temperature to High mode. Select START/STOP to begin preheating.

3. While unit is preheating, prepare guacamole by adding all ingredients to a blender and blitz to combine but leave small chunks.

4. Season with salt and pepper to taste. When the unit beeps to signify it is preheated, spray the grill plate with cooking spray and place the salmon in skin down.

5. Press Start/Stop button to begin. Close lid and cook for about 5 minutes. Flip the fish over after 5 minutes to ensure even cooking and charring on both sides.

6. Close the lid and cook for another 5 minutes. When the cooking process ends, flake up the salmon and serve hot in a tortilla with lettuce, tomatoes and guacamole.

7. Garnish with fresh coriander leaves, lime juice and/or cheese.

Grilled Scallops

Preparation time: 5 minutes

Cooking time: 20 minutes

Overall time: 25 minutes

Serves: 4 to 6 people

Recipe Ingredients:

- 25 large scallops (about 3 pounds)
- 5 tbsp. of olive oil
- 1 tsp. of salt
- 1 tsp. of black pepper
- 1 ½ tbsp. of lemon pepper

Cooking Instructions:

1. Pat dry each scallop and lay them on a tray. Sprinkle on some olive oil, coating scallops on all sides.

2. Season the scallops with salt, black pepper, and lemon pepper, making sure that the seasoning covers all sides. Refrigerate until ready to cook.

3. Grill for about 3 minutes on each side. Serve immediately.

Teriyaki Marinated Salmon

Preparation time: 5 minutes

Cooking time: 10 minutes

Overall time: 15 minutes

Serves: 2 to 4 people

Recipe Ingredients:

- 4 uncooked skinless salmon fillets, (6 ounces each) bag or container.
- 1 cup of teriyaki marinade

Cooking Instructions:

1. Move fillets around to coat evenly with sauce. Refrigerate for at least 1 hour and up to 12 hours. temperature to MAX, and set time to 8 minutes.

2. Select Start/Stop button to begin preheating. the grill grate, gently pressing them down to maximize grill marks.

3. Close hood and cook for about 6 minutes. There is no need to flip the fish during cooking.

4. Serve immediately and Enjoy!

VEGETARIAN RECIPES

Ninja Foodi Asparagus

Preparation time: 5 minutes

Cooking time: 15 minutes

Overall time: 20 minutes

Serves: 2 to 4 people

Recipe Ingredients:

- 2 lb. of asparagus, trimmed
- ½ tsp. of pepper
- 1 tsp. of salt
- ¼ cup of honey
- 2 tbsp. of olive oil
- 4 tbsp. of tarragon, minced

Cooking Instructions:

1. Combine the asparagus with oil, salt, pepper, honey, and tarragon and toss well.

2. Take Ninja Foodi Grill and arrange it over your kitchen platform, and open the top lid. Arrange the grill grate and close the top lid.

3. Press Grill function and select the Medium mode grill function. Adjust the timer to 8 minutes and then press Start/Stop.

4. Ninja Foodi will start pre-heating. It is preheated and ready to cook when it starts to beep. After you hear a beep, open the top lid.

5. Arrange the asparagus over the grill grate. Close the top lid and cook for about 4 minutes. Now open the top lid, flip the asparagus.

6. Close the top lid and cook for 4 more minutes. Serve warm.

Baked Asparagus

Preparation time: 5 minutes

Cooking time: 5 minutes

Overall time: 10 minutes

Serves: 2 to 4 people

Recipe Ingredients:

- 1 bunch of asparagus
- Olive oil
- Garlic granules
- Salt and pepper

Cooking Instructions:

1. Rinse and pat the asparagus dry. Break off the ends where the woody part starts.

2. They will break naturally at that point when you bend them. Add the asparagus to the basket of the Ninja.

3. Brush over the oil, add a sprinkling of garlic granules and season. Air fry at 200ºC for about 5 minutes flipping and checking midway.

4. Remove from the air fryer and serve immediately.

Tandoori Cauliflower

Preparation time: 5 minutes

Cooking time: 15 minutes

Overall time: 20 minutes

Serves: 2 to 4 people

Recipe Ingredients:

- 1 medium Cauliflower chopped into florets

For the marinade:

- ½ cup of Greek yoghurt
- 1 tablespoon of gram flour
- 4 cloves of garlic crushed
- 2 inch of ginger crushed
- 1 teaspoon of garam masala
- ½ teaspoon of red chilli powder
- ½ teaspoon of turmeric powder
- 1 teaspoon of curry powder
- 1 teaspoon of dried fenugreek (optional)
- Oil for brushing

Cooking Instructions:

1. Combine all the ingredients for the marinade in a large bowl.

2. Add the cauliflower florets and mix well. Put the florets into the air fryer basket and brush with oil.

3. Set to 180 and bake for about 16 to 18 minutes. Check midway and brush with more oil if necessary.

4. Serve immediately and Enjoy!

Harissa Lentil Veggie Burgers

Preparation time: 10 minutes

Cooking time: 20 minutes

Overall time: 30 minutes

Serves: 2 to 4 people

Recipe Ingredients:

- 1 (400g) tin brown lentils, well drained
- 1 ½ teaspoons of ras el hanout
- 2 tablespoons of rapeseed oil, divided
- 2 tablespoons of tomato paste
- 1 teaspoon of harissa paste
- 2 medium carrots, peeled and coarsely grated (to yield about 175g)
- 2 spring of onions, finely chopped
- ½ bunch (around 15g) of parsley, finely chopped
- ½ bunch (around 15g) of coriander, finely chopped
- 75g of panko crumbs
- Salt and pepper, to taste

Cooking Instructions:

1. Place three quarters of the drained lentils into a small food processor bowl along with one tablespoon of the oil, the tomato paste and harissa paste.

2. Process it to a smooth paste. Place the rest of the lentils in a bowl along with the processed paste and all remaining ingredients apart from the remaining oil.

3. Season to taste. Leave the mixture to sit for at least 5 minutes to allow the panko crumbs to absorb some of the moisture.

4. Form the mixture into 4 balls and then pat out into roughly 11cm burgers. Ensure that the edges are neat or they will cook unevenly and may burn.

5. Insert the grill plate in unit and close the hood. Select Grill function. Set temperature to High mode and set time to 8 minutes.

6. Select Start/Stop to begin preheating. While unit is preheating, brush the burger patties on both sides with the remaining oil.

7. Once the unit has beeped to signify it has preheated, place the 4 burgers on the grill plate and close hood.

8. After 4 minutes, open the hood and flip the burgers over and close the hood to finish cooking.

9. When cooking is complete, serve burgers in warmed pita pockets with salad or grilled red peppers, rocket and a tahini, garlic and lemon sauce.

10. Serve immediately and Enjoy!

Vegetable Lasagne

Prep Time: 15 minutes

Cooking time: 1 hour

Overall time: 1 hour 15 minutes

Serves: 7 to 9 people

Recipe Ingredients:

- 1 pack of dried lasagne pasta sheets
- 2 tablespoons of olive oil
- 1 courgette – finely diced
- 140g of broccoli – finely diced
- 1 red bell pepper – finely diced
- 1 yellow bell pepper – finely diced
- 140g of champignon mushrooms – finely diced
- 500g of tomato passata
- 100ml of water
- 2 garlic cloves - minced
- 1 teaspoon of oregano
- 1 teaspoon of basil
- ½ teaspoon of thyme
- ½ teaspoon of rosemary
- Salt and pepper to taste
- Cheese Layer
- 140g of grated hard cheese
- 140g of grated mozzarella
- 250ml of heavy cream
- Pinch of nutmeg
- Salt and pepper

Cooking Instructions:

1. In a large bowl add olive oil, 400g of tomato passata, garlic, oregano, basil, thyme, rosemary, salt and pepper and combine well.

2. Add all chopped vegetables to the tomato sauce and stir well. In a medium sized bowl combine hard cheese, mozzarella, heavy cream, nutmeg, salt and pepper.

3. Combine remaining tomato passata with water and spread out half of the mixture on the bottom of cooking pot.

4. Cover bottom of cooking pot with lasagne sheets and spread on ¼ of vegetable mixture evenly.

5. Layer with more pasta sheets and then spread 1/3 cheese mix. Repeat this until you have used all the vegetable and cheese mix.

6. Once you done, top your lasagne with remaining tomato water mix. Cover with a layer of baking paper and aluminum foil to prevent from drying out during baking.

7. Place pot with lasagne in the unit, select Bake function, set temperature to 170°C and set time to 45 minutes. Select Start/Stop to begin preheating.

8. Once unit has beeped to signify it has preheated, open and close lid to begin cooking.

9. When cooking has completed, remove pot from the unit and allow to rest for about 10 minutes. Serve hot with freshly grated parmesan and basil.

Vegetarian Pizza

Preparation time: 5 minutes

Cooking time: 10 minutes

Overall time: 15 minutes

Serves: 1 to 3 people

Recipe Ingredients:

For the Passata mix:

- 2 cloves of garlic, crushed
- Big pinch of dried oregano
- Salt and pepper, to taste

For the Pizza:

- 2 tablespoons of olive oil
- 1 pack of pre-made pizza dough
- 3 mushrooms, sliced finely
- 1 tablespoon of jalapeno slices
- ¼ red pepper cut into 1 inch squares
- 2 tablespoons of corn Kernels
- ½ small red onion sliced finely
- 2 handfuls of mozzarella and cheddar, combined

Cooking Instructions:

1. Combine the ingredients for the passata mix in a bowl.

2. Preheat the grill on the bake setting, using the high temperature. Roll out the pizza dough on a lightly floured surface. Poke holes all over with a fork.

3. Once the grill has pre-heated, place the dough into the grill and allow to bake on high for about 4 minutes.

4. Open the grill and carefully add the passata and vegetables on to the dough. Top with the cheese.

5. Bake for a further 5 minutes or until the cheese has melted. Serve immediately and Enjoy!

DESSERT RECIPES

Cheese and Chive Scones

Prep Time: 5 minutes

Cooking time: 30 minutes

Overall time: 35 minutes

Serves: 2 to 4 people

Recipe Ingredients:

- 270g of plain flour
- 6g of baking powder
- ½ teaspoon of salt
- 1 tablespoon of chives – finely chopped
- 40g of mature cheddar – grated
- 1 egg
- 100g of butter – softened
- 60g of crème fraiche
- 1 egg
- 1 tablespoon of milk for brushing

Cooking Instructions:

1. In a large bowl, add flour, baking powder, salt, chives and cheddar. Mix well and then add egg, softened butter and crème fraiche.

2. Combine as well as you can, then place on a clean surface and knead only until all loose flour has been worked into the dough.

3. Use cooking pot without grill plate or crisper basket installed. Close the lid. Select Bake, set temperature to 170°C and set time to 17 minutes.

4. Press Start/Stop to begin preheating. While unit is preheating, roll out the dough approximately 3cm thick.

5. Using a biscuit cutter cut out scones, rework left over dough and cut again. In a small bowl add egg and milk and combine well.

6. Brush top of scones with egg mix. Once unit beeps to signify it has preheated, lightly spray the pot with cooking spray and add scones.

7. Close hood to begin cooking. When cooking is complete, remove the scones and allow to cool down.

8. Serve with butter, chutney or as a side to soups and stews.

Crispy Cheesy Rice Balls

Preparation time: 5 minutes

Cooking time: 20 minutes

Overall time: 25 minutes

Serves: 2 to 4 people

Recipe Ingredients:

- 200g of cooked white rice
- 30g of grated hard cheese
- 50g of shredded mozzarella
- ½ teaspoon of garlic powder
- ¼ teaspoon of cayenne pepper
- 2 tablespoons of parsley
- ¼ teaspoon of nutmeg
- 1 egg
- Salt and pepper
- 1 egg
- 2 tablespoons of milk for egg wash
- 100g of breadcrumbs for breading

Cooking Instructions:

1. In a large bowl combine rice, hard cheese, mozzarella, garlic powder, cayenne pepper, parsley and egg.

2. Season with salt and pepper and mix well. Insert crisper basket in unit and close lid. Select AIR FRY, set temperature to 200°C and set time to 15 minutes.

3. Press Start/Stop button to begin preheating. While unit is preheating, divide rice "dough" into 8 equal parts and form balls. In a bowl combine egg and milk.

4. Whisk well to create egg wash. Place breadcrumbs in a different bowl to prepare for breading. First dunk rice balls in egg wash and then coat with breadcrumbs.

5. Once unit beeps to signify it has preheated, open lid and place all rice balls in the crisper basket.

6. Close lid to begin cooking. When cooking is complete, remove rice balls from unit and serve immediately with tomato sauce and salad.

Cinnamon Rolls with Pecans

Preparation time: 20 minutes

Cooking time: 1 hour 40 minutes

Overall time: 2 hours

Serves: 7 to 9 people

Recipe Ingredients:

- 400g of plain flour
- 200ml of warm milk
- 4g of dry yeast
- 40g of sugar
- 40g of softened butter
- 1 egg
- Pinch of salt

For the Filling:

- 40g of softened butter
- 40g of brown sugar
- 70g of finely chopped pecan nuts
- 1 tablespoon of cinnamon

Cooking Instructions:

1. In a medium sized bowl, add warm milk, sugar and yeast. Stir until yeast and sugar dissolved. Set bowl in a warm place and allow yeast to activate.

2. This will take about 2 to 3 minutes. Your yeast is activated when foam starts forming on top of mixture, add butter and egg.

3. In a large bowl, add flour, salt and pour in yeast mixture. Combine well, then place dough on a floured surface and knead for about 2 minutes or until it is smooth.

4. Place dough back in the bowl, cover with a wet tea towel and leave in a warm place. Allow to proof for 1 hour.

5. When dough has doubled in size, place on floured surface and roll out into an approximately 35x25cm rectangle. (cca 0,5cm thick).

6. Brush dough with melted butter, sprinkle with sugar, cinnamon and nuts. Tightly roll up dough starting at shorter side of the rectangle.

7. Carefully slice into 3cm wide slices and place cinnamon rolls on lightly floured tray and allow to rise for additional 20 minutes.

8. Ensure pot is installed but grill plate is removed. Select Bake, set temperature to 180°C and set time to 18 minutes.

9. Select Start/Stop to begin preheating. Once unit has beeped to signify it has preheated, open lid, lightly spray with baking spray and add cinnamon rolls.

10. Make sure you leave at least 1cm gap in between rolls as they will expand during cooking. Close lid to begin cooking.

11. When cooking has completed, remove cinnamon rolls and allow to cool down. Sprinkle with icing sugar.

12. Serve immediately and Enjoy!

Profiteroles

Preparation time: 10 minutes

Cooking time: 50 minutes

Overall time: 1 hour

Serves: 8 to 10 people

Recipe Ingredients:

For the choux pastry:

Wet ingredients:

- 150ml of milk (nut or cow's)
- 60g of unsalted butter (cubed)
- 1 tablespoon of coconut sugar
- 1 teaspoon of vanilla extract
- Pinch sea salt (fine)
- 2 medium eggs

Dry Ingredients:

- 135g of tapioca flour
- 1 tablespoon of coconut flour
- ½ teaspoon of baking powder

For the whipped coconut cream:

- 2 x 400ml tins of full fat coconut milk (refrigerated overnight)
- 1 tablespoon of maple syrup/agave nectar
- 1 teaspoon of vanilla extract

For the chocolate glaze:

- 100g of good quality dark chocolate (at least 70% cacao solids)
- 25g of unsalted butter

Cooking Instructions:

1. In a medium pan bring to the boil the milk, butter, coconut sugar, vanilla and sea salt.

2. Get together your dry ingredients into a bowl and put to one side whilst your milk is coming to the boil.

3. Remove the pan from the heat and beat in the tapioca flour, coconut flour, and baking powder rapidly with a wooden spoon until smooth.

4. The mixture should come away from the sides and form a nice 'ball' of choux dough, stirring continuously.

5. Leave to cool for a few minutes., whisk one egg then beat into the mixture, if needed whisk the second egg and carefully add a teaspoon at a time.

6. The mixture should reluctantly fall from the spoon. It should be stiff and not runny when you prod a wet finger into the dough it should leave a dent.

7. Place a round piping tip into a piping bag then fill the piping bag with the dough, push out any air and twist the end.

8. Place the piping bag into the refrigerator until needed. Place the air fryer basket into the pot of your Ninja Health Grill then close the lid and press Air Fry.

9. Set the temperature to 170°C and the time to 13 minutes. Wait for the unit to pre-heat.

10. Once pre-heated remove your piping bag from the refrigerator and pipe 5 circles carefully into the basket.

11. Make sure that they are an inch apart and about 5cm/2" in diameter. Using a wet finger gently press down any bumps.

12. Close the lid and return the piping bag to the refrigerator. After 10 minutes has passed open the lid and pierce each choux bun with a skewer.

13. Close the lid and cook for a further 3 minutes. Remove the basket with oven mitts then leave to cool for a couple minutes.

14. Lift the basket and using the back of a wooden spoon knock the bottom where any dough has cooked through the basket.

15. This will release them from the basket. Pierce the choux buns again and leave to cool on a wire wrack.

16. Repeat the process all over again for the remaining dough. Make your whipped coconut cream. Remove your tins of chilled coconut milk from the fridge.

17. Open the tins, poke a hole into the creamy top layer and drain out all of the water. Scoop out all of the solid cream into a large mixing bowl.

18. Add the remaining ingredients into the cream and whisk using large strokes to beat in as much air as possible. This will make the cream nice and fluffy and light.

19. Once the cream forms large stiff peaks it is done. Transfer into piping bags and use a large round or star tipped nozzle.

20. Place the chocolate over a double boiler on a low heat until melted then add the butter and stir until smooth.

21. Take your whipped cream and insert the piping tip into the bottom of the profiterole. Pipe in the cream until full.

22. Either dip each choux bun into your glaze or assemble onto a plate and drizzle all over.

23. Sprinkle over a little gold lustre dust for decoration if you wish. Serve immediately.

Lebkuchen Cake

Preparation time: 5 minutes

Cooking time: 30 minutes

Overall time: 35 minutes

Serves: 7 to 9 people

Recipe Ingredients:

- 350g of plain flour
- ¼ teaspoon of clove
- 170g of caster sugar
- 1 teaspoon of vanilla extract
- 1 teaspoon of baking powder
- 2 tablespoons of cocoa powder
- ½ teaspoon of ginger powder
- 1 teaspoon of cinnamon
- ¼ teaspoon of nutmeg
- ¼ teaspoon of allspice
- 3 eggs
- 200ml of oil
- 100ml of milk
- Cooking spray - for greasing

Cooking Instructions:

1. In a large bowl combine all dry ingredients and then add the eggs, oil and milk.

2. Mix thoroughly until well combined. Use cooking pot without grill plate or basket installed.

3. Close the lid and select BAKE function, set temperature to 170°C and set time to 30 minutes. Select Start/Stop button to begin preheating.

4. When the unit beep to signify it has preheated, open lid and lightly grease the pot with cooking spray or line with baking parchment.

5. Pour cake mixture into the pot and close lid to begin cooking. After 30 minutes, check whether cake is cooked through.

6. Cooking is complete when a wooden skewer inserted in the centre comes out clean. Carefully remove cooking pot and let cool down. Serve warm or cold.

Easy Lemon Cake

Preparation time: 5 minutes

Cooking time: 30 minutes

Overall time: 35 minutes

Serves: 7 to 9 people

Recipe Ingredients:

- 250g of plain flour
- 100g of sugar
- 4 teaspoons of vanilla extract
- 1 tablespoon of baking powder
- 2 eggs
- 100ml of oil
- 150g of yoghurt
- 1 lemon (zest & juice)

Cooking Instructions:

1. Select Bake function, set temperature to 160°C and time to 25 minutes. Press Start/Stop button and allow to preheat for about 5 minutes.

2. In a large bowl add sugar, vanilla sugar, lemon juice and zest, oil, yoghurt and eggs. Whisk until well combined.

3. Add flour and baking powder and mix thoroughly. Once you have a smooth runny dough use cooking spray to grease the cooking pan.

4. Once the unit beeps to signify it has preheated, our mixture into the cooking pan and place directly in pot, shut the lid and press Start.

5. When baking is complete, carefully remove the cooking pan and let the cake cool down.

6. Serve slightly warm with your favourite ice cream, jam or just simply cold as is.

Grilled Strawberry Shortcake Skewers

Preparation time: 20 minutes

Cooking time: 40 minutes

Overall time: 1 hour

Serves: 3 to 5 people

Recipe Ingredients:

- 1 box of classic white cake mix
- 1 cup of premade vanilla pudding (optional)
- Cooking spray
- 2 cups of strawberries, cut in half, stems removed
- 1/4 cup of granulated sugar
- 2 tbsp. of honey
- 5 skewers
- Whipped cream, for serving
- Vanilla ice cream, for serving

Cooking Instructions:

1. Mix cake batter according to the instructions on the box. Remove grill grate from unit and close hood.

2. Select Bake and set temperature to 325°F, and set time to 40 minutes. Select Start/Stop button to begin preheating.

3. While the unit is preheating, liberally coat the Ninja (or an 8-inch baking pan) with cooking spray and pour batter into the pan.

4. When the unit has beeps to signify it has preheated, place the pan in the pot. Close hood and cook for about 40 minutes.

5. Meanwhile, place the strawberries in a mixing bowl and toss them with sugar until well coated.

6. Let them sit for about 5 to 10 minutes, then add honey and mix well to coat and set strawberries aside.

7. When cooking is complete, allow the cake to cool for 15 to 20 minutes, then remove it from the pan and use a serrated knife to cut it into 2" x 2" cubes.

8. Assemble the skewers alternating between cake cubes and strawberries. Reserve the liquid from the strawberries. Insert grill grate in unit and close hood.

9. Select Grill, set temperature to High, and set time to 6 minutes. Select Start/Stop to begin preheating.

10. While the unit is preheating, spray each skewer with cooking spray. When the unit has beeps to signify it has preheated, place skewers on the grill grate.

11. Close hood and cook for about 3 minutes. After 3 minutes, flip skewers over, close hood, and cook for 3 more minutes.

12. When cooking is complete, transfer skewers to a serving plate. Spoon strawberry liquid over the top and serve with whipped cream and/or vanilla ice cream.

Grilled Apple & Raspberry Pie

Preparation time: 10 minutes

Cooking time: 40 minutes

Overall time: 50 minutes

Serves: 6 to 8 people

Recipe Ingredients:

- Juice of 1 lemon
- 8 cups of cold water
- 8 Granny Smith apples, peeled, cored cut in quarters, divided
- 1 ½ cups of raspberries, rinsed
- ¼ cup plus 1 tbsp. of dark brown sugar, divided
- ¼ cup plus 1 tbsp. of granulated sugar, divided
- ½ tsp. of ground cinnamon
- ½ tsp. of ground ginger
- 3 tbsp. of all-purpose flour
- ½ cup of applesauce
- 1 frozen pie crust, defrosted
- Ice cream, optional, for serving

Cooking Instructions:

1   Combine lemon juice, water, and apple slices in a bowl. Let slices soak for about 10 minutes.

2   Remove them from the water and pat very dry. Insert grill grate in unit and close hood. Select Grill, set temperature to Max mode.

3   Set time to 8 minutes. Select Start/Stop to begin preheating. While unit is preheating, dice 8 of the apple slices and set them aside.

4   In a mixing bowl, toss remaining slices with 1 tablespoon dark brown sugar and 1 tablespoon granulated sugar, covering all slices evenly.

5   When the unit beeps to signify it has preheated, place slices tossed with sugar on the grill grate and cook for about 8 minutes. Do not flip slices during grilling.

6   Meanwhile, combine raspberries, remaining dark brown sugar, remaining granulated sugar, cinnamon, ginger, flour, applesauce, and diced apples in a mixing bowl.

7   When cooking is complete, gently fold grilled apples into the ingredients in the mixing bowl.

8   Pour mixture into the Ninja (or an 8-inch baking pan), spreading evenly. Lay pie crust over the top and pinch around the edges to ensure it adheres to pan.

9   Using a knife, cut several Xs in the dough so steam can escape during baking.8 Remove grill grate from unit.

10   Select Bake, set temperature to 350F, and set time to 20 minutes. Select Start/Stop button to begin preheating.

11   When the unit beeps to signify it has preheated, place pan directly in pot. Close hood and cook for about 20 minutes.

12   When cooking is complete, allow pie to cool for about 20 minutes before serving warm with ice cream, if desired

BEEF, PORK AND LAMB
Flank Steak Skewers-Rojo Filete

Preparation time: 10 minutes

Cooking time: 45 minutes

Overall time: 55 minutes

Serves: 2 to 4 people

Recipe Ingredients:

- 2 lb. of flank steak cut against the grain into strips
- 6 cloves of minced garlic
- ¼ cup of red wine vinegar
- 2 tablespoons of avocado oil or oil of choice-high smoke point oil
- 2 tablespoons of tomato paste
- 1 ¼ teaspoons of kosher salt
- 1 teaspoon of black pepper

Cooking Instructions:

1. Place steak into freezer. for about 45 minutes to 1 hour. While steak is in freezer make the sauce.

2. In a bowl whisk together minced garlic, vinegar, oil, salt, pepper, tomato paste and set it aside. You can preheat the Ninja Foodi Grill.

3. Place the ceramic bowl/liner into NF grill then place grill grate into ceramic bowl and close lid. Don't forget the metal mesh in lid to protect heating element.

4. Then turn it on Ninja Foodi Grill, select grill Max which is 510°F the press start. Its most likely going to take longer than 8 minutes to slice them.

5. mix meat with sauce/marinade and place them on skewers. I just let the Ninja Foodi grill preheat longer.

6. Remove meat from freezer, using a sharp knife you are going to cut against the grain at a 45°C angle and make ¼-inch thick slices and place into a large bowl.

7. When finished slicing meat. Take the sauce whisk again if needed and pour over flank steak and mix to coat the meat evenly.

8. With the enclosed metal skewers and bamboo skewers if needed. Place the meat on the skewers in a ribbon like fashion.

9. When you have 5 of the skewers done you can raise the lid on Ninja Foodi Grill and place them on grill grate. The meat should make a nice sizzling sound.

10. Close the lid and the timer will start. The Ninja Foodi Grill defaults to 10 minutes. After 2-3 minutes raise lid and turn over skewers and close lid.

11. They should take maybe 3-4 minutes longer. Total cook time should be 7-10 minutes depending on how you want them done.

12. When done remove from Ninja Fooodi grill and place on a plate. These can be served with rice, pita pocket, wrap, roasted vegetables. Enjoy!

Apple and Sage Stuffed Pork Tenderloin

Preparation time: 10 minutes

Cooking time: 35 minutes

Overall time: 45 minutes

Serves: 2 to 4 people

Recipe Ingredients:

- 1 whole pork tenderloin
- 1 apple, shredded
- 100g of bacon (about 8-10 rashers)
- 10 sage leaves, finely chopped
- 1 tablespoon of butter
- 1 tablespoon of mustard
- 1 tablespoon of honey
- Salt and pepper to taste

Cooking Instructions:

1. Prepare your tenderloin by spreading it out on a cutting board and cutting 2-3 cm deep pocket through the whole length.

2. In a small bowl combine mustard and honey. Brush the mixture on the meat including the pocket.

3. Combine shredded apple, finely chopped sage, butter, salt and pepper. Place the stuffing into the meat pocket.

4. Use the Ninja Health Grill cooking pot without the grill plate or crisper basket installed, close the lid.

5. Select Roast, set temperature to 240°C and set time to 30 minutes. Press Start/Stop to begin preheating.

6. While the unit is preheating, wrap the tenderloin with bacon. Be sure to wrap the bacon tightly enough not to fall apart while cooking. Secure ends with a skewer.

7. When the unit beeps to signify it has preheated, place the tenderloin in the cooking pot. Close the lid and allow to cook for about 30 minutes.

8. Open the lid every 10 minutes and brush the meat with the remaining honey and mustard glaze.

9. When cooking is complete, carefully remove the tenderloin from the unit and let rest for about 5 minutes.

10. Serve hot with side of mashed potatoes and veggies

Ninja Foodi Grill Lasagna

Preparation time: 20 minutes

Cooking time: 55 minutes

Overall time: 1 hour 15 minutes

Serves: 2 to 4 people

Recipe Ingredients:

- ½ lb. of ground beef/hamburger
- ½ lb. Italian sausage
- ¼ teaspoon of Italian seasoning
- ¼ teaspoon of garlic powder
- 6-oven ready lasagna. noodles
- 16 ounces of ricotta cheese
- 2 eggs
- ¼ cup of parmesan cheese grated
- 1 cup of mozzarella cheese shredded
- ½ teaspoon of kosher salt
- ½ teaspoon of black pepper
- 1 tablespoon of dried parsley
- ¼ teaspoon of garlic powder
- ½ teaspoon of Italian seasoning
- 1 ½ cups of mozzarella cheese shredded this is for the top of lasagna
- 24 ounces of spaghetti sauce Use your favorite sauce

Cooking Instructions:

1   Turn on Ninja Foodi and select Sear/Sauté function and set High mode and press start. Allow this to warm up and get hot.

2   When Ninja Foodi or pan on stove is hot add both ground beef and sausage, used wooden spoon to break up meat into small pieces.

3   Add the ¼ teaspoon of garlic powder and ¼ teaspoon of Italian seasoning. Cook/brown meat up. making sure it is broken into small. pieces.

4   This will take 5-7 minutes. While the meat I browning you. can mix. up the ricotta filling.

5   In a large bowl add ricotta, eggs, parmesan cheese, mozzarella cheese, parsley, garlic powder, salt and black pepper. Mix with a spatula or wooden spoon to combine well.

6   You can check on meat mixture while you making the filling. After mixing set to the side. After meat mixture is done cooking, pour this mixture in a large bowl.

7   Add the 24 ounces jar of sauce and mix together and set to the side. Line bottom of pan with oven ready lasagna noodles.

8   Cover entire bottom and try not to overlap that much. As this will increase the bake time. Ensure the noodle cooked through.

9   Nest take half the ricotta mixture and spread over the top of the lasagna noodles. Next take half of the meat mixture and spread on top of ricotta mixture.

10 Then place another single layer of lasagna noodles, ricotta gain and finally topping with meat mixture.

11 Then top with the 1 ½ cups of mozzarella cheese. Take a piece of parchment paper and cut it to the size of your pan or use a parchment round.

12 Cover the top of the pan and then cover with aluminum foil. Make sure the foil is tucked under the pan.

13 As we don't want the aluminum foil to be pulled up by the fan in the Ninja Foodi Grill. Preheat your Ninja Food Grill to 350°F.

14 You will need something to raise. the ninja foodi pan off the bottom of the NinjaFoodi grill bottom.

15 Use a 9-inch silicone round and the use a rack forms my dehydrator rack. But you can use whatever you have on hand.

16 The Ninja Foodi grill has a roasting rack but this makes it too tall to close lid. But you could use the roasting rack if you have shorter pan.

17 After it preheats add your lasagna. to the Ninja Foodi Grill. Then place a heavy fork, spoon, knife

18 That weighs at least 3 ounces and place that on top of the aluminum foil to. hold it down-this is a very important step.

19 Close lid and set time for about 55 minutes. Check for doneness at the 35-minute mark. If not done return lasagna to Ninja Foodi Grill and continue baking until done.

20 Make sure heavy utensil is on top of aluminum foil. When done let sit to cool and firm up a little.

Marinated London Broil

Preparation time: 15 minutes

Cooking time: 2 hours

Overall time: 2 hours 15 minutes

Serves: 2 to 4 people

Recipe Ingredients:

- 1½ pounds of London broil
- ¼ cup of red wine vinegar
- 1 tablespoon of olive oil
- 1½ tablespoon of spicy mustard
- 2 cloves of garlic minced
- 1 tablespoon of Worcestershire sauce
- 2 teaspoon of rosemary fresh and chopped
- 1 teaspoon of sea salt
- 1 teaspoon of onion powder
- 1 teaspoon of dried thyme leaves
- ½ teaspoon of black pepper

Cooking Instructions:

1 Trim up the steak if there is any visible fat. Tenderize each side with a meat tenderizer. Mince the garlic cloves and finely chop the rosemary if using fresh.

2 Combine all the marinade ingredients into a large plastic, sealable bag. Or use a shallow container with a lid.

3 Add the steak and seal the bag. Mix the marinade all around so the ingredients combine with each other. Squeeze the air out of the bag.

4 Refrigerate for about 2 to 4 hours. Remove the steak from the fridge, leave it in the bag and let it sit at room temperature for about 30 minutes.

5 Remove the steak from the bag and blot off the marinade. Preheat the indoor grill on max grill. When it says Add Food, lay the steak on the grill surface.

6   Press the steak down onto the grill surface. Grill on max grill for about 4 minutes and then flip. Grill on max, grill another 2 to 4 minutes for medium rare.

7 Remove from grill and let the steak rest for about 5 to 10 minutes. Slice thinly across the grain. Serve and Enjoy!

Sirloin Steak

Preparation time: 5 minute

Cooking time: 10 minutes

Overall time: 15 minutes

Serves: 1 to 3 people

Recipe Ingredients:

- 2 sirloin steaks
- Spray oil
- 1 tablespoon of alt
- 1 teaspoon of ground pepper

Cooking Instructions:

1 Preheat the unit. Close lid and set to grill on High.

2 Once preheated, add the steak, spray with oil on both sides and set timer for about 4 minutes.

3 Sprinkle over the salt and pepper. Close and cook. Flip and cook for a further 2 minutes.

4 Allow to rest before serving.

Grilled New York Strip Steak with Asparagus

Preparation time: 10 minutes

Cooking time: 15 minutes

Overall time: 25 minutes

Serves: 2 to 4 people

Recipe Ingredients:

- 2 uncooked New York strip steaks (14–16 ounces each)
- 2 tbsp. of canola oil, divided
- Kosher salt, as desired
- Ground black pepper, as desired
- 1 bunch of asparagus, trimmed

Cooking Instructions:

1   Brush each steak on all sides with ½ tablespoon of canola oil, then season with salt and pepper, as desired.

2   Toss asparagus with remaining canola oil, then season with salt and pepper, as desired.

3   Insert grill grate in unit and close hood. Select Grill function, set temperature to High mode, and set time to 12 minutes.

4   Select Start/Stop to begin preheating. When the unit beeps to signify it has preheated, place steaks on grill grate, gently pressing them down to maximize grill marks.

5   Close hood and cook for about 4 minutes. After 4 minutes, flip steaks. Close hood and continue cooking for 4 more minutes, or until internal temperature reaches 125°F.

6   Remove steaks from grill and let it rest 5 minutes; they will continue to cook to a food-safe temperature while resting.

7   Use a cooking thermometer to ensure a food-safe temperature has been achieved. While steaks are resting, place asparagus on grill grate.

8   Close hood and cook for about 4 minutes. When cooking and resting are complete, slice steaks and serve with asparagus.

Frozen Southwest Ribeye Steak with Peppers and Onions

Preparation time: 10 minutes

Cooking time: 20 minutes

Overall time: 30 minutes

Serves: 1 to 3 people

Recipe Ingredients:

- 1 tsp. of smoked paprika
- ½ tsp. of garlic powder
- ½ tsp. of onion powder
- ½ tsp. of cumin
- ½ tsp. of kosher salt, plus more as desired
- ½ tsp. of ground black pepper, plus more as desired
- 1 frozen ribeye steak, up to 18 ounces
- 1 tbsp. plus 1 tsp. of canola oil, divided
- 1 bell pepper, cut in 1-inch slices, seeds and ribs removed
- 1 small white onion, peeled, sliced in 1-inch rings
- ¼ cup of prepared fajita sauce

Cooking Instructions:

1   In a small bowl, mix paprika, garlic powder, onion powder, cumin, 1/2 teaspoon salt, and ½ teaspoon of ground black pepper and set aside.

2   Insert grill grate in unit and place Ninja Veggie Tray on grill grate and close hood. Select Grill function, set temperature to Medium mode and set time to 20 minutes.

3   Select Start/Stop to begin preheating. While unit is preheating, brush ribeye with 1 tablespoon oil and season with salt and pepper, as desired.

4   In a bowl, toss peppers and onions with remaining teaspoon oil and spice mix. Once the unit has beeped to signify it has preheated.

5   Place ribeye on the grill grate, gently pressing it down to maximize grill marks. Close the hood and cook for about 10 minutes.

6   After 10 minutes, baste ribeye liberally with fajita sauce. Flip ribeye using rubber-tipped tongs, then baste it again with fajita sauce.

7   Place peppers and onions in Ninja Veggie Tray. Close hood to continue cooking. After 5 minutes, stir peppers and onions with a rubber-tipped spatula.

8   If desired, baste steak with any remaining fajita sauce. Close hood and cook for 3 more minutes.

9   After 3 minutes, check ribeye for desired doneness. If necessary, cook up to 2 more minutes or until desired doneness is achieved.

10 When cooking is complete, remove ribeye and vegetables from grill and serve.

Reverse Sear Horseradish Roast Beef

Preparation time: 10 minutes

Cooking time: 50 minutes

Overall time: 1 hour

Serves: 2 to 4 people

Recipe Ingredients:

- ¼ cup of creamy horseradish
- 1 tbsp. of Dijon mustard
- 1 tbsp. of garlic, minced
- 2 tbsp. of fresh herbs, such as rosemary and parsley
- 1 tbsp. of kosher salt
- 1 tsp. of ground black pepper
- 1 eye of round beef roast (up to 2 pounds), maximum 3 inches thick

Cooking Instructions:

1 In a small bowl, combine all ingredients except beef. Using a knife, score beef by making shallow diagonal cuts across all surfaces of beef.

2 This will help the sauce adhere to beef. Coat beef on all sides with horseradish sauce, rubbing sauce into score marks made by knife. Plug temperature probe into unit.

3 Insert Ninja Roasting Rack in pot and close hood. Select Roast and set temperature to 250°F. Select the TEMP iQ and set temperature to 105°F.

4 Select Start/Stop to begin preheating. While unit is preheating, insert probe into center of beef.

5 Once the unit beeps to signify it has preheated, place beef on the roasting rack. Close hood over the probe cord.

6 When the unit beeps and the probe icon flashes to signify cooking is complete, select Start/Stop.

7 Then select Roast and set temperature to 500°F. Select TEMP iQ and set temperature to 125°F. Close hood and select Roast again to skip preheat.

8 When "Add Food" appears on the display, open and close hood and continue cooking until the unit beeps and the probe icon flashes to signify cooking is complete.

9   Remove beef from unit and allow it to rest up to 10 minutes before serving. To check the internal temperature at any time.

10 Press TEMP iQ for 2 seconds until the screen displays the internal temperature. Serve immediately and Enjoy!

Bacon-Wrapped Tenderloin Filets

Preparation time: 10 minutes

Cooking time: 15 minutes

Overall time: 25 minutes

Serves: 2 to 4 people

Recipe Ingredients:

- 8 strips of uncooked bacon
- 4 center-cut beef tenderloin filets (8 ounces each)
- Toothpicks, as necessary
- 2 tbsp. of canola oil, divided
- Kosher salt, as desired
- Ground black pepper, as desired

Cooking Instructions:

1   Wrap 2 strips of bacon around the entire outside of each filet. Use toothpicks to secure bacon in place.

2   Rub all sides of wrapped filets with canola oil, then season with salt and pepper, as desired. Install grill grate in unit and close hood.

3   Select Grill function, set temperature to High mode, and set time to 12 minutes. Select Start/Stop to begin preheating.

4   When the unit beeps to signify it has preheated, place filets on the grill grate. Gently press them down to maximize grill marks, then close the hood and cook for 6 minutes.

5   After 6 minutes, flip filets. Close lid to continue cooking for about 6 minutes or until the filets' internal temperature reads 130°F on a food thermometer.

6   Remove filets from unit. They will continue to cook to a food-safe temperature while they are resting.

7   Allow filets to rest for 10 minutes before serving—this will allow the juices to redistribute evenly through the filets.

Ninja Grill Steak

Preparation time: 12 minutes

Cooking time: 2 hour minutes

Overall time: 2 hours 12 minutes

Serves: 1 to 4 people

Recipe Ingredients:

- 2 steaks
- 1 tbsp. of Kosher salt
- ¼ tsp. of corn starch
- ½ tsp. of chili powder
- 2 tsp. of brown sugar
- ¼ tsp. of onion powder
- 1 tsp. of black pepper
- ¼ tsp. of Tumeric
- ½ tsp. of smoked paprika

Cooking Instructions:

1   Start by mixing up all your steak seasonings in a bowl. Once steaks are rubbed down with the spices on all sides, you will wrap or cover and store in the fridge.

2   Store for about 30 minutes to 2 hours. The longer you store the more flavor. Preheat your Ninja Foodi Grill to the highest grill setting and allow it to fully preheat.

3   This takes about 8-12 minutes. Once the preheat is done take your steaks and place them on the grill. You will cook your steaks to the doneness you desire.

4   Once your steaks are done, allow resting on a plate for about 5 minutes that is tented in aluminum foil. This will help lock in juices from the steak.

5   Once you have waited serve up your Ninja Foodi grill steaks

Steak and Potatoes

Preparation time: 15 minutes

Cooking time: 45 minutes

Overall time: 1 hour

Serves: 2 to 4 people

Recipe Ingredients:

- 4 potatoes russet
- 3 steak, timings shared below
- ¼ cup of avocado oil
- 2 tablespoons of steak seasoning
- 1 tablespoon of sea salt

Cooking Instructions:

1   Wash potatoes, dry, and poke with a fork all over them. Rub avocado oil all over each one so they are well saturated. Sprinkle salt on outsides and put into air fryer basket.

2   Close lid and set to 400°F, select the air fry function, for about 35 minutes. Flip, then cook for an additional 10 minutes until middle is fork tender when poked.

3   Remove potatoes and cover with foil to keep warm. Remove air fryer basket and replace with grill piece inside machine.

4   Close lid and set to grill, 500°F for about 10 minutes. Allow to preheat. Sprinkle both sides of steak with seasoning and press down so it sticks well.

5   When Ninja Foodi Grill is done preheating it will say lift add food. Add steaks now. Sirloins we cooked 8 minutes flipping halfway through.

6   Cook filet for about 6 minutes flipping after 4 minutes. Remove once you feel it is done to your liking.

7   Allow to rest for at least 5 minutes to maintain juiciness before cutting.

Pot Roast in the Ninja Foodi Grill

Preparation time: 10 minutes

Cooking time: 6 hours

Overall time: 6 hours 10 minutes

Serves: 4 to 6 people

Recipe Ingredients:

Seasoning Blend

- 2 teaspoons of thyme leave, dried
- 2 teaspoons of sea salt
- 1 teaspoon of black pepper
- 1 teaspoon of garlic powder
- 1 teaspoon of onion powder
- ½ teaspoon of red pepper flakes optional

Pot Roast Ingredients:

- 2 tablespoons of avocado oil
- 4 pounds of Chuck Roast
- 1 onion
- 4 cups of beef stock divided
- ¼ cup of flour optional for gravy *see post for details
- 6 carrots
- 6 small potatoes

Cooking Instructions:

1 Add the oil to the inner pan of the Indoor Grill and preheat on high grill mode at 500°F. Combine the seasoning in a bowl and rub onto both sides of the chuck roast.

2 When the grill has preheated and says, Add Food, place the roast on the bottom of the inner pan.

3 Close the lid and grill on high mode for about 5 minutes. Flip and grill another 5 minutes. Cut your onion into chunks and add to the pan.

4 Pour in 2 cups of beef stock and select the Roast function on 250°F and set the time for 3 hours.

5 Flip the roast every hour or so, but this isn't completely necessary. After the 3 hours, remove the meat.

6   Make the gravy by combining the remaining beef stock and flour with some of the liquid in the pan into a large glass Mason jar or another glass container with a lid.

7   Shake until it is well combined, pour into the pan. Put the roast in along with the vegetables and set the grill to the roast setting on 250°F for another 3 hours.

8   The total cook time will depend on your roast, so start checking it after the 1st hour and give it a flip.

9   It is ready when the meat is fork tender and the vegetables are done to your liking. Serve & Enjoy!

Sausage & Pepper Grinders

Preparation time: 10 minutes

Cooking time: 25 minutes

Overall time: 35 minutes

Serves: 4 to 6 people

Recipe Ingredients:

- 2 bell peppers, cut in quarters, seeds and ribs removed
- 1 white onion, peeled, sliced in 1-inch rings
- 2 t bsp. of canola oil, divided Kosher salt, to taste
- Ground black pepper, to taste
- Raw sausages (4 ounces each), like hot Italian or Bratwurst
- Hot dog buns
- Condiments, as desired

Cooking Instructions:

1   Insert grill grate in unit and close hood. Select Grill, set temperature to LOW, and set time to 12 minutes. Select Start/Stop to begin preheating.

2   While unit is preheating, toss bell peppers and onions with oil, salt, and black pepper. When the unit beeps to signify it has preheated.

3   Place peppers and onions on the grill grate and close hood and cook for about 12 minutes without flipping.

4   While peppers and onions are cooking, plug temperature probe into the unit. After 12 minutes, transfer peppers and onions to a medium mixing bowl.

5   Insert probe into center of one sausage Place sausages on the grill grate, then select TEMP iQ and set temperature to 160°F.

6   Close hood over the probe cord. Meanwhile, gently break up the grilled onions into individual rings and mix them with the peppers.

7   When the unit beeps and the probe icon flashes to signify cooking is complete, open hood and remove sausages from grill.

8   While wearing oven mitts, remove probe from sausage. Spread any desired condiments on the buns, then place sausages in buns.

9   Top each liberally with peppers and onions and serve.

Grilled New York Strip Steak & Asparagus

Preparation time: 10 minutes

Cooking time: 15 minutes

Overall time: 25 minutes

Serves: 2 to 4 people

Recipe Ingredients:

- 2 uncooked New York strip steaks
- Ground black pepper, as desired   (14–16 ounces each)
- 1 bunch asparagus, trimmed
- 2 tbsp. of canola oil, divided
- Kosher salt, as desired

Cooking Instructions:

1   Brush each steak on all sides with ½ tablespoon of canola oil, then season with salt and pepper, as desired.

2   Toss asparagus with remaining canola oil, then season with salt and pepper, as desired. Plug temperature probe into unit. Insert grill grate in unit and close hood.

3   Select Grill function and set temperature to High mode. Select TEMP iQ and set the desired internal cook temperature.

4   Select Start/Stop to begin preheating. While unit is preheating, insert probe into the center of the thickest steak.

5   Once the unit beeps to signify it has preheated, place steaks on grill grate, gently pressing them down to maximize grill marks. Close hood over the probe cord.

6   When the screen reads 90°F, open hood and flip steaks. Close hood and continue cooking until the unit beeps and the probe icon flashes to signify cooking is complete.

7   Remove steaks from unit and allow them to rest. Leave probe in steak and connected to the unit to monitor internal temp of steak while it rests.

8   While steak is resting, place asparagus on grill grate and close hood. Select Grill function, set temperature to High mode, and set time to 4 minutes.

9   Select Start/Stop to begin cooking. To check the steak's temp at any time, press TEMP iQ for 2 seconds until the screen displays the internal temp.

10 The screen will then go back to showing the countdown timer. When cooking and resting are complete, remove probe. Slice steak and serve with asparagus.

Steak & Vegetable Kebabs

Preparation time: 10 minutes

Cooking time: 15 minutes

Overall time: 25 minutes

Serves: 2 to 4 people

Recipe Ingredients:

- 2 New York strip of steaks (10–12 oz. each), cut in 2-inch cubes
- White button mushrooms, cut in half, stems removed
- 1 bell pepper (green, yellow, or red), cut in 2-inch pieces
- 1 small white onion, peeled, cut in quarters, petals cut in 2-inch pieces
- Kosher salt, as desired
- Ground black pepper, as desired
- Steak seasoning, as desired

Cooking Instructions:

1   Insert grill grate in unit and close hood. Select Grill function, set temperature to High mode, and set time to 12 minutes.

2   Select Start/Stop button to begin preheating. While unit is preheating, assemble the skewers in this order until they are almost full: steak, mushroom, bell pepper, onion.

3   Ensure ingredients are pushed almost completely down to the end of the skewers. Season skewers liberally with salt, pepper, and steak seasoning.

4   When the unit beeps to signify it has preheated, place skewers on the grill grate. Close hood and cook for about 8 minutes without flipping.

5   After 8 minutes, check steak for desired doneness, cooking up to 4 more minutes if desired. When cooking is complete, serve immediately.

Coffee-Crusted Bone-In Ribeye

Preparation time: 10 minutes

Cooking time: 25 minutes

Overall time: 35 minutes

Serves: 2 to 4 people

Recipe Ingredients:

- 2 tbsp. of ground chipotle pepper
- 2 tbsp. of dark coffee grinds
- 1 tbsp. of kosher salt
- 2 tsp. of ground black pepper
- 1 tsp. of garlic powder
- 1 tsp. of onion powder
- ½ tsp. of mustard powder
- ½ tsp. of ground ginger
- 1 tbsp. of canola oil1 bone-in beef ribeye (2 pounds), maximum 2 inches thick

Cooking Instructions:

1. In a small bowl, mix all ingredients except canola oil and beef. Brush beef with canola oil and then coat beef liberally on all sides with coffee rub.

2. Plug temperature probe into unit. Insert grill grate in unit and close hood. Select Grill and set temperature to HIGH mode.

3. Select the TEMP iQ and set the desired internal cook temperature. Select Start/Stop button to begin preheating.

4. While unit is preheating, insert probe into center of beef close to but not touching the bone. Once the unit beeps to signify it has preheated.

5. Place beef on the grill grate, gently pressing down to maximize grill marks. Close hood over the probe cord.

6. When the display reads 110°F, open hood and flip beef. Close hood and continue cooking until the unit beeps, the probe icon flashes to signify cooking is complete.

7. Remove beef from unit and allow it to rest up to 10 minutes before serving. It will continue cooking to the desired doneness even after removed from the grill.

8. Leave probe in beef and connected to the unit to monitor internal temp of beef while it rests.

9. To check the internal temp at any time, press TEMP iQ for 2 seconds until the screen displays the internal temp.

Reverse Sear Horseradish Roast Beef

Preparation time: 10 minutes

Cooking time: 40 minutes

Overall time: 50 minutes

Serves: 2 to 4 people

Recipe Ingredients:

- ¼ cup of creamy horseradish
- 1 tbsp. of Dijon mustard
- 1 tbsp. of garlic, minced
- 2 tbsp. of fresh herbs, such as rosemary and parsley
- 1 tbsp. of kosher salt
- 1 tsp. of ground black pepper
- 1 eye of ground beef roast (up to 2 pounds), maximum 3 inches thick

Cooking Instructions:

1. In a small bowl, combine all ingredients except beef. Using a knife, score beef by making shallow diagonal cuts across all surfaces of beef.

2. This will help the sauce adhere to beef. Coat beef on all sides with horseradish sauce, rubbing sauce into score marks made by knife.

3. Plug temperature probe into unit. Insert Ninja® Roasting Rack in pot and close hood, make sure the grill grate or air crisp basket is removed from the unit.

4. Select Roast and set temperature to 250°F, there is no time adjustment available or necessary when using the TEMP iQ function.

5. Select the TEMP iQ and set temperature to 105°F. Select Start/Stop button to begin preheating.

6. While unit is preheating, insert probe into center of beef. Once the unit beeps to signify it has preheated, place beef on the roasting rack.

7. Close hood over the probe cord. When the unit beeps and the probe icon flashes to signify cooking is complete, select Start/Stop button.

8. Then select Roast and set temperature to 500°F. Select TEMP iQ and set temperature to 125°F. Close hood and select Roast again to skip preheat.

9. When Add Food appears on the display, open and close hood and continue cooking until the unit beeps and the probe icon flashes to signify cooking is complete.

10. Remove beef from unit and allow it to rest up to 10 minutes before serving, it will continue cooking to the desired doneness even after removed from the grill.

11. To check the internal temp at any time, press TEMP iQ for 2 seconds until the screen displays the internal temp.

Grilled Flank Steak

Preparation time: 10 minutes

Cooking time: 15 minutes

Overall time: 22 minutes

Serves: 2 to 4 people

Recipe Ingredients:

- 500g of flank steak
- 2 cloves of garlic, peeled and minced
- 3 tablespoons of olive oil
- 3 tablespoons of soy sauce
- 2 tablespoons of honey
- 2 tablespoons red wine
- ¼ teaspoon of lemon pepper
- Cooking spray or rapeseed oil for brushing

Cooking Instructions:

1. Using a sharp knife, score the flank steak across the grain 1-2cm apart. Combine all other ingredients in a long shallow dish and mix well.

2. Add the steak to the marinade and coat evenly. Allow to marinate refrigerated for at least 2 hours, or up to 1 day.

3. Insert the Grill Plate into unit and close the lid. Select Grill function and set temperature to High mode, then press Start/Stop button to begin preheating.

4. When the unit beeps to signify it has preheated, open the lid and lightly spray or brush the grill with rapeseed oil.

5. Place the flank steak onto the grill, close lid and set cook time for about 12 minutes. At the 6-minute mark, flip the steak over to grill on the other side.

6. When cook time is finished, remove the steak to a plate, and cover with foil. Allow meat to rest for about 5 to 10 minutes.

7. Using a sharp knife, thinly slice the steak across the grain. it will be a delicious medium rare. Serve immediately and enjoy!

Lamb Kebabs

Preparation time: 10 minutes

Cooking time: 40 minutes

Overall time: 50 minutes

Serves: 6 to 8 people

Recipe Ingredients:

- 2 teaspoons of cumin seeds
- 1 kg of minced lamb (not too lean)
- ¼ red onion, roughly chopped
- 3 green chillies
- 10 coriander stalks
- 5 garlic cloves
- 1-inch ginger crushed
- 1 teaspoon of red chilli powder
- 1 teaspoon of garam masala
- 1 teaspoon of black pepper
- 1.5 teaspoon of salt
- 40g of cheddar cheese, grated (optional)
- 8 wooden skewers, soaked for a few hours
- Oil for brushing

Cooking Instructions:

1   In a dry frying pan over a medium heat, dry fry the cumin seeds for a minute. Watch them carefully to make sure they don't burn.

2   Remove from the pan and add to the bowl of a food processor, along with the remaining ingredients. Process very quickly to combine.

3   Don't over mix, this is just to bring the ingredients together. Alternatively mix by hand. Portion the mixture into 8 balls and then squeeze onto the presoaked skewers.

4   Put them in the fridge for about 30 minutes. Insert the grill plate in the unit and close the lid.

5   Select Grill, set temperature to the highest setting and set timer for about 12 minutes. Brush the kebabs with oil and place on the grill plate.

6   Close the lid and turn after 6 minutes. Check at 10 minutes to make sure they aren't browning too much.

Indian Masala Lamb Chops

Preparation time: 10 minutes

Cooking time: 15 minutes

Overall time: 20 minutes

Serves: 6 to 8 people

Recipe Ingredients:

- 2kg of lamb chops
- 200g of natural yoghurt
- 80ml of oil
- 1 teaspoon of salt
- 1 teaspoon of kashmiri chilli powder
- ¾ teaspoon of paprika powder
- ½ teaspoon of turmeric powder
- ½ teaspoon of chilli flakes
- 1 teaspoon of garlic powder
- ¾ teaspoon of ginger powder
- 1 teaspoon of onion powder
- 1 teaspoon of coriander powder
- 1 teaspoon of cumin powder
- ¾ teaspoon of garam masala powder
- ½ teaspoon of ground black pepper

Cooking Instructions:

1 Marinate chops in a large bowl with all the ingredients listed for about 2 hours.

2 Insert grill plate in unit. Select grill and set temperature to medium. Set time to 20 minutes.

3 Select Start to pre heat. Once ready, open and add 4 chops. Close lid to begin cooking. Flip after 5 minutes and close lid.

4 Check at 4 minutes and cook for an additional minute if needed. Continue with remaining chops.

5 Serve immediately and Enjoy!

SNACKS AND APPETIZERS RECIPES

Pickle Spears with Special Sauce

Preparation time: 15 minutes

Cooking time: 20 minutes

Overall time: 35 minutes

Serves: 2 to 4 people

Recipe Ingredients:

- 12 dill pickle spears
- 1 cup of all-purpose flour
- 2 eggs
- 1 egg white
- 1 box (4 ½ oz.) of seasoned coating mix
- Cooking spray
- 2 tbsp. of ketchup
- 2 tbsp. of yellow mustard
- 2 tbsp. of mayonnaise

Cooking Instructions:

1   Add flour to a shallow bowl. Add eggs and egg white to a second shallow bowl and whisk thoroughly for about 60 seconds.

2   In a third shallow bowl, add seasoned coating mix. Pat pickle spears dry. Toss 2 pickles in flour until evenly coated.

3   Gently tap them off to remove excess flour, then coat in egg wash. Transfer pickles to bread crumbs, tossing well to evenly coat. Place pickles on a plate.

4   Repeat with remaining pickles and place plate of pickles in freezer for 30 minutes. Insert crisper basket in unit and close hood.

5   Select Air Fry, set temperature to 375°F, and set time to 18 minutes. Select Start/Stop button to begin preheating.

6   Remove pickles from freezer and spray on all sides with cooking spray. When the unit beeps to signify it has preheated, arrange pickles evenly in basket.

7   Close hood to begin cooking for about 9 minutes. Meanwhile, mix together ketchup, mustard, and mayonnaise in a small bowl to make sauce and set aside.

8 After 9 minutes, flip pickles using rubber-tipped tongs. Close hood to resume cooking for about 7 minutes.

9 After 7 minutes, check pickles' doneness. If desired, close hood and continue cooking up to 2 more minutes.

10 When cooking is complete, remove pickles using rubber-tipped tongs and serve with immediately with sauce.

Spiced Grilled Grapefruit

Preparation time: 5 minutes

Cooking time: 5 minutes

Overall time: 10 minutes

Serves: 2 to 4 people

Recipe Ingredients:

- 2 ruby grapefruits
- 2 tablespoons of raw cane sugar
- 1 teaspoon of ground cinnamon
- ¼ teaspoon of ground cardamom
- Pinch sea salt

Cooking Instructions:

1 Add in the grill plate and set the Ninja Foodi Grill to Grill on High mode.

2 Set the time to 7 minutes and let the unit pre-heat. Cut the grapefruits in half then sprinkle the sugar on top of the open fruit.

3 Stir together the spices then sprinkle over evenly, followed by a pinch of sea salt on each.

4 Once the unit prompts to add food, carefully place each grapefruit half cut side down. Close the unit and leave to cook for the allocated time.

5 Once cooking is complete, remove using silicone tongs and serve immediately.

Dried Apples

Preparation time: 15 minutes

Cooking time: 7 hours

Overall time: 7 hours 15 minutes

Serves: 2 to 4 people

Recipe Ingredients:

- 4 apples – cored and thinly sliced (2-3mm)
- Lemon juice from ½ lemon
- ½ teaspoon of cinnamon
- 3 tablespoons of powdered sugar

Cooking Instructions:

1   In a large bowl mix apple slices, lemon juice, cinnamon and sugar.

2   Evenly spread out seasoned apple sliced on dehydrating rack. Insert dehydrating rack into unit and close lid.

3   Select Dehydrate, set the temperature to 60°C and timer for 7 hours. Press Start/Stop button to begin dehydrating process.

4   Once unit beeps to signify that the dehydrating process has finished, remove dehydrating rack from the unit and let cool down.

5   Serve as is or store in air tight container for up to one week.

Apple Strudel

Preparation time: 10 minutes

Cooking time: 35 minutes

Overall time: 45 minute

Serves: 2 to 4 people

Recipe Ingredients:

- 4 apples – peeled and grated
- 1 tablespoon of lemon juice
- ½ teaspoon of cinnamon
- ¼ teaspoon of nutmeg
- 60g of raisins
- 40g of brown sugar
- 275g of ready rolled puff pastry
- 1 egg for brushing
- 2 tablespoons of breadcrumbs

Cooking Instructions:

1 Place grated apples in a strainer, pour over lemon juice and squeeze lightly to remove excess juice from apples.

2 Place apples in a large bowl, add sugar, cinnamon, nutmeg, raisins and combine well. Insert pot in the unit and close lid.

3 Select Bake, set the temperature to 170°C and time to 25 minutes. Press Start/Stop button to begin preheating.

4 While unit is preheating, spread puff pastry out, sprinkle the middle with breadcrumbs which will help absorb juices from the apples during baking.

5 Place apple mixture down the middle over the breadcrumbs. Cut sides of pastry unto approximately 1 cm wide strips.

6 Beginning at the top, fold left strip at a 45° angle over the apple mixture, then do the same with the right strip.

7 Continue repeating this until you have "braided" all the strips and tuck the bottom strips that are sticking out underneath the strudel.

8 Once unit beeps to signify it has preheated, line the pot with baking paper and place strudel in the pot diagonally.

9   Close lid and cook for the first 10 minutes. Add egg to a cup and whisk. When there is only 10 minutes left on the timer, open lid and brush strudel with the egg.

10 Close lid to continue cooking. When cooking is complete, carefully remove Strudel from the unit and allow to cool down.

11 Serve slightly warm with vanilla sauce or your favourite ice cream.

Toffee Popcorn

Preparation time: 5 minutes

Cooking time: 5 minutes

Overall time: 10 minutes

Serves: 4 to 6 people

Recipe Ingredients:

- 125g of popcorn kernels
- 115g of butter
- 115g of sugar
- 4 tablespoons of golden syrup

Cooking Instructions:

1   Insert basket, close lid and select pre heat.

2   Select Air fry function, set temperature to 180ºC and set time to 4 minutes. Melt butter, sugar and syrup in a large pot over medium heat.

3   Bring to a simmer and allow to bubble for about 4 to 5 minutes over medium low heat. Add the popcorn to the pot and stir through.

4   Serve immediately and Enjoy!

Buffalo Chicken Wings

Preparation time: 10 minutes

Cooking time: 30 minutes

Overall time: 40 minutes

Serves: 2 to 4 people

Recipe Ingredients:

- 2 lb. of chicken wings, rinsed, patted dry
- 2 tbsp. of canola oil
- ½ cup of prepared Buffalo sauce, plus more as desired

Cooking Instructions:

1   In a large mixing bowl, toss chicken wings with canola oil until evenly coated. Insert crisper basket in unit.

2   Select Air Fry, set temperature to 390°F, and set time to 26 minutes. Select Start/Stop button to begin preheating.

3   When the unit beeps to signify it has preheated, place wings in basket, spreading out evenly. Close hood and cook for 12 minutes.

4   After 12 minutes, stir wings with rubber-tipped tongs. Close hood and cook for 12 more minutes. After 12 minutes, remove wings from basket.

5   For additional crispiness, cook wings up to an additional 2 minutes. When cooking is complete, transfer wings to a large mixing bowl.

6   Pour buffalo sauce over them, and use rubber-tipped tongs to mix wings with sauce. Serve immediately.

Roasted Rainbow Cauliflower

Preparation time: 15 minutes

Cooking time: 20 minutes

Overall time: 35 minutes

Serves: 2 to 4 people

Recipe Ingredients:

- ½ head (approx. 6 oz.) white cauliflower, cut in 2-inch florets
- ½ head (approx. 6 oz.) purple cauliflower, cut in 2-inch florets
- ½ head (approx. 6 oz.) yellow cauliflower, cut in 2-inch florets
- 3 tbsp. of extra virgin olive oil
- Kosher salt, as desired
- Ground black pepper, as desired

Sauce:

- 1 tbsp. of Asian chili paste
- ¼ cup of extra virgin olive oil
- 2 tbsp. of rice wine vinegar
- 3 tbsp. of honey
- 1 tbsp. of soy sauce
- 1 tbsp. of fresh cilantro, minced
- ¼ cup of roasted peanuts, coarsely chopped
- 1 tbsp. of sesame seeds

Cooking Instructions:

1. Insert crisper basket in unit and close hood.

2. Select Air Fry, set temperature to 390°F, and set time to 20 minutes. Select Start/Stop button to begin preheating.

3. Combine cauliflower, olive oil, salt, and pepper in a large mixing bowl, tossing well to evenly distribute the oil and seasonings.

4. When the unit beeps to signify it has preheated, place cauliflower in the basket. Close hood and cook for about 9 minutes.

5. After 9 minutes, stir cauliflower with silicone tipped tongs or a spatula. Close hood to continue cooking for 9 more minutes.

6. Meanwhile, if desired, stir together all sauce ingredients in a large mixing bowl. After 9 minutes, check cauliflower for doneness and crispiness.

7. If desired, cook up to 2 more minutes. When cooking is complete, toss cauliflower in the sauce, and serve.

Grilled Tomato Salsa

Preparation time: 15 minutes

Cooking time: 10 minutes

Overall time: 25 minutes

Serves: 2 to 4 people

Recipe Ingredients:

- 5 Roma tomatoes, cut in half lengthwise
- 1 red onion, peeled, cut in quarters
- 1 jalapeño pepper, cut in half, seeds removed
- 1 tbsp. of kosher salt
- 2 tsp. of ground black pepper
- 2 tbsp. of canola oil
- 1 bunch fresh cilantro, stems trimmed
- 3 cloves of garlic, peeled
- 2 tbsp. of ground cumin
- Juice and zest of 3 limes

Cooking Instructions:

1   In a large bowl, combine tomatoes, onion, jalapeño pepper, salt, and black pepper with canola oil.

2   Mix well to ensure vegetables are coated with oil and seasonings. Insert grill grate in unit and close hood.

3   Select Grill, set temperature to Max mode, and set time to 10 minutes. Select Start/Stop button to begin preheating.

4   When the unit beeps to signify it has preheated, place vegetable mixture on the grill grate. Close hood and cook for about 5 minutes.

5   After 5 minutes, flip vegetables. Close hood and cook for the remaining 5 minutes. When cooking is complete, remove mixture from unit and allow to cool.

6   Transfer cooled mixture to a food processor. Add cilantro, garlic, cumin, and lime juice and zest. Pulse until desired consistency is reached.

7   Serve immediately, or chill in refrigerator first.

MEXICAN STREET CORN

Preparation time: 10 minutes

Cooking time: 15 minutes

Overall time: 25 minutes

Serves: 2 to 4 people

Recipe Ingredients:

- 4 ears corn, shucked
- 2 tbsp. of canola oil, divided
- Kosher salt, as desired
- Ground black pepper, as desired

Sauce:

- 1 cup of cotija cheese, grated, plus more for garnish
- ¼ cup of mayonnaise
- ¼ cup of sour cream
- Juice of 2 limes
- 1 tsp. of garlic powder
- 1 tsp. of onion powder
- ¼ cup of fresh cilantro, chopped

Cooking Instructions:

1 Insert grill grate in unit and close hood. Select Grill functions, set temperature to Max mode, and set time to 12 minutes.

2 Select Start/Stop button to begin preheating. While unit is preheating, brush each ear of corn with ½ tablespoon of canola oil.

3 Season corn with salt and pepper, as desired. When the unit beeps to signify it has preheated, place corn on grill grate and close hood and cook for about 6 minutes.

4 After 6 minutes, flip corn. Close hood and continue cooking for the remaining 6 minutes.

5 Stir together all sauce ingredients in a mixing bowl. When cooking is complete, coat corn evenly with sauce.

6 Garnish with additional cotija cheese and serve immediately.

Grilled Watermelon

Preparation time: 5 minutes

Cooking time: 10 minutes

Overall time: 15 minutes

Serves: 2 to 4 people

Recipe Ingredients:

- 6 watermelon slices, each measuring
- 3 inches of across and 1-inch thick
- 2 tbsp. of honey

Cooking Instructions:

1 Insert grill grate in unit and close hood. Select Grill functions, set temperature to Max mode, and set time to 2 minutes.

2 Select Start/Stop button to begin preheating. While unit is preheating, brush watermelon slices liberally on both sides with honey.

3 When the unit beeps to signify it has preheated, place watermelon on grill grate. Press down gently to increase contact with grate.

4 Close hood and grill for 2 minutes without flipping. When cooking is complete, serve immediately.

Honey & Herb Charred Carrots

Preparation time: 5 minutes

Cooking time: 20 minutes

Overall time: 25 minutes

Serves: 2 to 4 people

Recipe Ingredients:

- 1 tbsp. of honey
- 1 tsp. of kosher salt
- 2 tbsp. of melted butter
- 6 medium carrots, peeled, cut in lengthwise
- 1 tbsp. of fresh parsley, chopped
- 1 tbsp. of fresh rosemary, chopped

Cooking Instructions:

1 Insert grill grate in unit and close hood. Select Grill function, set temperature to Max mode, and set time to 10 minutes.

2 Select Start/Stop button to begin preheating. In a small bowl, stir together honey, salt, and melted butter.

3 Coat carrots with the honey butter, then rub evenly with the fresh herbs. When the unit beeps to signify it has preheated, place carrots on the center of the grill grate.

4 Close hood and cook for about 5 minutes. After 5 minutes, turn the carrots. Close hood and cook for the remaining 5 minutes.

5 When cooking is complete, serve immediately and Enjoy!

Acknowledgement

In preparing the "Ninja Foodi Grill Cookbook 2021", I sincerely wish to acknowledge my indebtedness to my husband for his support and the wholehearted cooperation and vast experience of my two colleagues - Mrs. Catherine Long, and Mrs. Alexander Bedria.

EMILY COOK

CPSIA information can be obtained
at www.ICGtesting.com
Printed in the USA
LVHW100851210121
676968LV00003B/294